An OPUS book

The Problems of Evolution

Mark Ridley is a Junior Research Fellow of New College, Oxford. He is also the author of *The Explanation of Organic Diversity* (OUP 1983) and many articles and reviews on the subject of evolution.

Mark Ridley

The Problems of Evolution

Oxford   New York

OXFORD UNIVERSITY PRESS

1985

Oxford University Press, Walton Street, Oxford OX2 6DP

London New York Toronto
Delhi Bombay Calcutta Madras Karachi
Kuala Lumpur Singapore Hong Kong Tokyo
Nairobi Dar es Salaam Cape Town
Melbourne Auckland

and associated companies in
Beirut Berlin Ibadan Mexico City Nicosia

Oxford is a trade mark of Oxford University Press

British Library Cataloguing in Publication Data
Ridley, Mark
The problems of evolution.—(Opus)
1. Evolution
I. Title   II. Series
575   QH366.2
ISBN 0–19–219194–2
ISBN 0–19–289175–8 Pbk

Library of Congress Cataloging in Publication Data
Ridley, Mark.
The problems of evolution.
(An OPUS book)
Bibliography: p.
Includes index.
1. Evolution.   I. Title.   II. Series: OPUS.
QH366.2.R526   1985   575   84-27300
ISBN 0–19–219194–2
ISBN 0–19–289175–8 (pbk.)

Set by Promenade Graphics, Cheltenham
Printed in Great Britain by
Richard Clay (The Chaucer Press) Ltd.
Bungay, Suffolk

Preface

As I have studied the Darwinian controversies of recent years, I have repeatedly seen them misrepresented as if they signified something broader and more threatening than I believe they are. Science journalists have been the main culprits. Shifts of emphasis have been exaggerated into 'paradigm shifts'; interesting, but relatively minor, hypotheses have been blown up into attacks on Darwin himself. The controversies will look rather different in this book. Actually, there are several distinct controversies, taking place in different spheres, and each (it seems) with the manners appropriate to its media. Outside biology is the creationism controversy, in which the validity of evolution itself is being challenged; scientific evidence is strangely treated here, and I do not suppose that my first chapter will persuade any creationists to alter their position; but I do still think it is worth setting out what the reasons are for thinking that evolution is true. Then there are controversies, such as that of molecular evolution, in which only professionals take part. And finally there are controversies, like those of palaeontology and classification, uneasily situated in both the popular and technical theatres.

I hope that this work will provide an introduction to those controversies; but it is designed with a broader aim in mind. Instead of discussing only the modern controversy, I have preferred to introduce the problems of evolution as if they were timeless, and to concentrate only on the relative merits of their various proposed solutions. In so doing, I have covered nearly all modern controversy and in a way that I hope will reveal its context in the theory of evolution as a whole.

I designed the book to resemble Bertrand Russell's *The Problems of Philosophy*. Russell, however, enjoyed at least one advantage in his subject matter. European philosophy, as we know from Whitehead's famous remark, is a series of footnotes to Plato.

Because philosophers do not solve their problems, their subject can easily be introduced as a set of problems that they have always been discussing. Science is not like that. Evolutionary biology is not a set of footnotes to Darwin. Darwin's solution to the problem of heredity, for instance, was simply wrong. I have not filled up any of my space with it. The main text does presuppose some small acquaintance with the science of genetics—but not much, for I have fitted that necessary material in a short appendix. In an appendix I could treat it (as is only appropriate) as a fact rather than a problem.

Although evolutionary biology has advanced since Darwin, he had nevertheless set out nearly all the main questions of the subject, together with their possible answers—to an extent that can still astonish an evolutionary biologist looking at the Master's words for the first time. Evolutionary biology can be thought of as a set of Great Questions. I have concentrated on ten of them, and have so ordered them that we start with those that (I believe) have been effectively answered and progress towards those that have not. The truth of evolution and its explanation, in the case of adaptation, by natural selection (Chapters 1–4) are both settled. The mechanism of evolution of non-adaptive traits (which we meet at the end of Chapter 4) and of molecules (Chapter 5) is less certain. The relation of evolution and classification (Chapter 6) is a subject on which I happen to have strong opinions; but it is at present an open question, even if I think it should not be. The questions of why living things exist in such groups as species (Chapter 7) and of how one species splits into two (Chapter 8) are still undecided. We also do not know for sure whether evolution proceeds in relative jumps at speciation (Chapter 9), although some facts are available. We finish with a discussion of the mechanism of larger-scale evolutionary changes (Chapter 10); and must end on a speculative note because, although we can discuss several hypothetical mechanisms of macro-evolution, we lack the evidence to support an opinionated conclusion.

MARK RIDLEY

Contents

List of Figures

1 Is Evolution True?

The first problem of evolution is whether it is itself true. Although almost all biologists are now agreed on the answer, it cannot be taken for granted. Both common sense and many of the high authorities of history (if not of the present) testify to the immutability of species. To take common sense, species do seem—if you do not look too far and wide—always to reproduce their kind: cows reproduce cows, robins robins, and oaks oaks; cows do not reproduce robins, or even horses. What facts and arguments can disprove the authority of common sense and history?

We are after arguments that will choose between evolution and the fixity of species. But whether any particular argument can do so depends on exactly what theories are being considered. There are three main alternatives, defined by their answers to two questions (Figure 1): whether species are immutable and how many independent origins of life there have been. We shall take evolution to mean that all modern species have descended from a single common ancestral species; species have thus changed in appearance as they have descended and diversified through time. According to the theory of evolution, life originated only once and species are not immutable. The present diversity of forms has been produced from one ancestor by the splitting of species.

It could be that species do change, but that life has originated more than once. Species might change into new species without splitting; the single lineage might last indefinitely, without ever going extinct. The theory of Lamarck was something like that. He denied that species ever go extinct, and thought that species slowly change into more progressive forms. To make an extreme alternative to evolution, we could hypothesize that life has originated as many times as there are modern species: then each

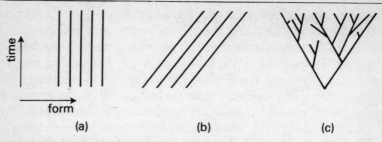

Fig. 1. Three theories of the history of life.
(a) separate creation (b) transformism (c) evolution.

modern species would be the descendant (in more or less modified form) of a different ancestor. The history of life would have
been independent creations (perhaps all at the same time, perhaps
at different times) followed by transformation, rather than
immutability, within each lineage. We shall call this hypothesis
transformism.

There are other alternatives. The obvious one, from its histori-
cal importance, is a literal reading of the biblical Book of Genesis.
There it is asserted that man was created as man. The species did
not start as a pre-cellular set of molecules that could hardly be
recognized as alive. Genesis (on this literal reading) certainly
denies both parts of the evolutionary hypothesis, transformation
of species and the common ancestry of life. But we shall not use
Genesis as an alternative to evolution. It is too easy to refute without any biological evidence. The most conclusive argument
against Genesis is its chronology: Genesis does not suggest an age
of the Earth as old as 3,500 million years; indeed, the usual funda-
mentalist figure is about 6,000 years, although the creationists of
Arkansas in 1981 preferred 'a relatively recent inception of the
earth and living kinds'. That 'relatively recent' was chosen to contradict the scientific chronology, as does the figure of 6,000 years.
The radio-isotopic evidence of the antiquity of the earth, therefore, provides a decisive argument against Genesis. Let us leave it
at that, and move on to another alternative.

An alternative to evolution does not have to assert that the
Earth is less old than it is. It could just assert that species do not

change through time, that all species have in the past always looked as they do now; and that species have separate origins. Let us call this alternative the theory of separate creation. Something very like it was held by the geologist Charles Lyell in the early editions of his work *The Principles of Geology* (1830–3). Separate creation is a different theory from the biblical alternative to evolution; and the main argument against Genesis does not harm it.

We now have, apart from Genesis, three theories of the history of life. They differ in their answers to the questions of whether species are fixed in appearance or can change over the generations; and whether there has been a single ancestor of modern species or several. *Separate creation* states that species do not change and that there were as many origins of species as there have been species; what we may call *transformism* states that species do change, but that there have been several origins of life; and *evolution* states that species change, and split into more than one species, and that present-day species are the descendants of a single ancestor.

We have three main kinds of evidence to test the three theories. The first is the observation of evolution on a small scale; the second is the argument from classification, which concerns certain patterns in the diversity of life; and the third comes from the fossil record. We shall take them in that order.

The best evidence of evolution would be to see it in action. This has been achieved under both natural and artificial conditions. Naturally occurring evolutionary change is studied by the school of ecological genetics, which has many discoveries to its credit. The best known is the case of the peppered moth in Great Britain. This moth exists in two main forms, a dark one and a light one. Before the Industrial Revolution the light form was much the commoner; but through the nineteenth century, in industrial areas, the dark form gradually increased in numbers, to become the commoner form. A comparable degree of evolutionary change has been studied in many other species. In all of them, the appearance of the species has changed through time: they have evolved and been seen to evolve. Similar changes can be produced artificially. A new generation that differs from its predecessor can easily be produced by breeding selectively from certain forms in a population. If one breeds, for instance, from only the larger mice of a population, the next generation will have a larger average weight. The evolutionary change can be watched as it takes place. The observation will favour the theories of evolution and of transformism, but will count against separate creation.

The usual objection to examples such as these is that they are on too small a scale. A critic of evolution will admit small changes within a species, but deny that these changes could accumulate sufficiently to produce large-scale change. No one, he will declare, has ever seen the origin of a new species. But this is an error. The exact form of the error will depend on the concept of species that the critic holds. There are two main concepts: morphological and reproductive. According to the morphological species concept, species are defined by the similarity of appearance of their members. According to the reproductive concept, the species is defined by interbreeding: if two individuals can breed together, they are members of the same species; if they cannot (unless they are the same sex, or reproductively immature) they are members of different species. The varieties of dogs would serve as an example of artificially created new species in the morphological sense. The differences between extreme varieties of dogs—such as the Pekinese and the Great Dane—are much larger than the normal morphological differences between species. An African hunting dog and a wolf, for instance, are classified in separate subfamilies, but they look more alike than a Pekinese and a Great Dane.

New species have been created in the reproductive sense too. Most examples come from agriculture and horticulture. Hundreds of new plant species have been experimentally manufactured. Because the same method is nearly always used, a single example can stand for them all. Let us consider the best-known case, the flowerpot primrose *Primulus kewensis*. Its origins are as follows. Two primrose species, *P. verticillata* and *P. floribunda*, were hybridized together. They do not normally interbreed, but can be forced to, at a low rate. The hybrid offspring are sterile, as inter-species hybrids usually are. But there is a method by which the hybrids can be made fertile among each other. If the numbers of their hereditary structures called chromosomes can be caused to double, the hybrids can reproduce. (Doubling of chromosome numbers can be encouraged by certain chemicals, such as colchicine.) *P. verticillata* and *P. floribunda* have 18 chromosomes each, as do their sterile hybrids. But a hybrid with 36 chromosomes can breed. They can breed among each other, but not with either of the parent species. The hybrids, once they have been made fertile, are a new reproductive species. They can interbreed with other members of their own species, but not with members of any other species.

The flowerpot primrose is not a freak example. Hundreds of strains of common garden flowers, such as tulips, irises, crocuses, are artificial hybrids. Nor is this method of forming new species confined to the horticulturist's experimental garden. It is thought to be how many new species of plants arise in nature. The evidence is this. If we count the number of chromosomes in the members of the different species of a genus of flowering plants, we often find that the numbers are simple multiples ($2n$, $4n$, $8n$, etc.) of a basic number (n) of chromosomes. The obvious interpretation is that the different species originated by hybridization followed by doubling of the chromosome numbers. If we assume this interpretation to be correct (which is probably not always a valid assumption), we can estimate the number of species of plants that have originated by hybridization: the estimate is that between one third and one half of all species of plants have.

The best check of the idea that a species has originated by hybridization of two other species is to try to re-create the candidate hybrid by experimentally crossing the candidate parent species. This has been done in several cases. The first success, by Müntzing in 1930, was the artificial creation of the mint *Galeopsis tetrahit* from two other mint species, *G. pubescens* and *G. speciosa*.

So species are not immutable. New species can be artificially made from old ones. We can also see the species category being violated in nature. If the same species is studied in different places, it will be found to differ slightly from place to place. The spatial rate of change is (usually) insensibly slow, but the extreme forms can be so different that they were classified (before the geographic connection was known) as different species. Normally it is not known whether the extremes do behave as separate reproductive species, because they are too far apart ever to try to mate. But sometimes the geographic extremes do meet. Then we can see whether they behave as separate species. This is the case where the geographic distribution is in the form of a ring. The distribution of the herring gull around the North Pole forms a ring. As we look at the herring gull, moving westwards from Great Britain to North America, we see gulls that are recognizably herring gulls, although they are a little different from the British form. We can follow them, as their appearance gradually changes, as far as Siberia. At about this point in the continuum the gull looks more like the form that in Great Britain is called the lesser black-backed gull. From Siberia, across Russia, to northern Europe, the gull gradually changes to look more and more like the British lesser black-backed gull. Finally, in Europe, the ring is complete; the two geographically extreme forms meet, to form two perfectly good species: the herring and lesser black-backed gull can be both distinguished by their appearance and do not naturally interbreed.

The gulls are not the only example, but they are enough to make the point. They show that the species barrier is not fixed in nature. They count against the theory of the separate creation of species, and for both transformism and evolution. If observation were confined to northern Europe, the two gulls would look like two ordinary species. One might imagine that they had separate origins. But what of all the insensible gradations between the two around the North Pole? A creationist could hardly argue that *all* the gradations were separately created, for if the argument is pursued it must lead to the absurd conclusion that all individuals were separately created, because all individuals differ to some extent. We know that conclusion to be absurd, for individual organisms are not separately created out of the air or in the ground; they originate in the reproduction of other individuals. At some arbitrary point between individual differences and the species difference, the creationist will have to declare that up to this point normal individual variation is permitted, but beyond it something altogether different happened. At that point some process of the separate origin of species did its work.

The error of the creationist argument is in this case obvious. If the differences within the herring gull species were evolutionary, the difference between the herring gull and lesser black-backed gull must be as well. If evolution can produce the difference between gulls in Canada and eastern Siberia, it can surely also produce the difference between gulls in east and in west Siberia. But in many other cases, if less obviously, the creationist error is the same. There is a continuous gradation from individual variation, through geographical variation, through such levels as the subspecies, through the species level, and up through the Linnaean hierarchy of genus, family, order, class, phylum. It is difficult to argue convincingly that evolution takes place up to some point in this hierarchy (such as within the species), but separate creation is necessary to produce larger differences. The degrees of difference are a continuum. If any point on the continuum is chosen as the limit of evolution, a paradox immediately arises. If evolution can produce all the changes up to that point, why can it not produce the tiny change from one side of the point to the other?

We only have direct observation, in nature and the laboratory, of evolution on the small scale. We can see the species barrier being broken. But to extend the principle to greater degrees of difference we need the philosophical principle of uniformitarianism. Uniformitarianism (in the required form) simply states that a process that we have seen in operation for a short period of time could have operated for longer, to produce proportionally larger effects. Although it can be tested, it is not really an empirical principle: it should be trusted more for its logical force. It is needed in all science. It is the principle by which we extend theories that have been tested on the small scale to explain observations on a much larger scale. Gravity, for instance, was extended (by Newton) from its well-confirmed small-scale operation to the motions of heavenly bodies. No one has ever directly tested that stars pull each other in the way that an apple is pulled to the earth: we trust uniformitarianism. If uniformitarianism is denied, all of science becomes impossible. There is nothing scientifically special or peculiar in the dependence of the theory of evolution on uniformitarianism. Those who affect to be sceptical about evolution because of its dependence on uniformitarianism should reflect on how destructive a position they have adopted.

Thus far the evidence has been more convincing against the theory of separate creation than of transformism. We have shown that species are not fixed in form; but we have yet to show that all life shares a single common ancestor. But we have not run out of evidence yet. Let us consider next how the diversity of life can be classified into a hierarchy. The species *Homo sapiens* is (at successively more and more inclusive levels) an anthropoid ape (family), a primate (order), a mammal (class), a chordate (phylum), an animal (kingdom). All species can be classified in an analogous hierarchy. The hierarchy can be interpreted as a temporal hierarchy of evolutionary descent, as the first animal evolved before the first vertebrate, which evolved before the first mammal, and so on down to the level of species.

But that is merely an interpretation. There is more to the argument for evolution than that. Any set of objects, whether or not they originated in an evolutionary process, can be classified hierarchically. Chairs, for instance, are independently created; they are not generated by an evolutionary process: but any given list of chairs could be classified hierarchically, perhaps by dividing them first according to whether or not they were made of wood, and then according to their colour, by date of manufacture, and so on. The fact that life can be classified hierarchically is not, in itself, an argument for evolution.

The argument for evolution comes from a particular property of the classificatory hierarchy, the kind of traits that define it. Species are classified together if they share certain traits. The important point about these traits is that they are what are often called homologies. Homologies (for our present purposes) are traits that are similar between species, but do not have to be because of functional necessity. The similar shape of sharks and dolphins, for instance, is not homologous. Although they look similar, the similarity is demanded by their similar way of life. Now, traits like the body shape of sharks and dolphins are not used in classification. Biological classifications are defined instead by similarities that are not functionally necessary, homologies as we are here using that term. The ear-bones of mammals are an example of a homology. They are homologous with some of the jaw-bones of reptiles. The ear-bones of mammals did not have to be formed from the same bones as form the jaw of reptiles; but in fact they are. If reptiles and mammals evolved separately, we should not expect to find this similarity. But if mammals evolved from reptiles, we should expect to find otherwise unintelligible similarities. Clearly the ear-bones evolved from the jaw-bone. The traits that define biological classifications are of the same kind as the bones of the jaw in reptiles and ears in mammals: they are homologies. The fact that species share homologies is an argument for evolution, for if they had been created separately there would be no reason why they should show homologous similarities.

The sheer number of homologous similarities among species makes a powerful argument for evolution. Many of what are often presented as separate arguments for evolution reduce to the general form of the argument from homology. Take the famous case of the Galapagos finches. There are, on the different islands of that archipelago, 14 different species of finch. The 14 species fill many of the roles we should expect (on another continent) to be played by other, unrelated birds. One of them, for instance, is a woodpecker-finch. It has evolved a long woodpecker-beak but not a long tongue; it therefore makes use of a twig, held in its beak, to extract insects from bark. Another is a warbler-finch, which is so like a warbler that it was classified as one for over a century before Darwin made his collections. But closer study revealed that it was really a finch.

If all the 14 species had been created separately, why are they all finches? If a woodpecker will serve as a woodpecker in the rest of the world, why should it be a finch that acts as a woodpecker on the Galapagos? But the facts make sense if the species all evolved from a common ancestor. If a single finch colonized the Galapagos and then speciated into the present 14 forms, we should expect them all to be finches: they all descended from a finch. The fact that they are finches is known from all the homologies that define a finch. If they had been created separately, we should not expect them to share all the finch-homologies. The woodpecker would be the same as a woodpecker anywhere else in the world; it would not have finch-defining traits. The Galapagos finches, therefore, provide evidence of evolution.

The argument for evolution from homology does not, as did the direct observation of experimental and natural evolution, depend on uniformitarianism. It is an argument of a different kind. It states that there are properties of the diversity of life that can only be understood if that diversity was produced by evolution from a common ancestor. It does not merely prove that evolution can make new species; it proves that whole classes and phyla must have originated from a common ancestor. In the extreme case of universal homologies, which are shared by all species, the argument from homology suggests that all life on earth has a single ancestor.

The outstanding example of a universal homology is the genetic code. Bodies are built from the hereditary material, DNA, by the translation of a sequence made up of four bases, which are symbolized by the four letters A, C, G, and T. A triplet of these bases specifies an amino acid; a sequence of triplets specifies a sequence of amino acids; a sequence of amino acids makes up a protein; and (roughly speaking) bodies are built of many different proteins. What matters here is that the code, although it is arbitrary, is known to be universal. It is arbitrary in the same sense that human language is arbitrary: there is nothing about a horse that demands it must be specified by that sequence of five letters: any sequence of letters would do. The genetic code has the same property. The amino acid called glycine happens to be specified in all species by the base triplet GGC; but there is nothing (so far as we know) about glycine which demands that it be specified by this triplet rather than any other. Now, if different species had been created separately, we should be very surprised if they had all been built with exactly the same genetic code. It would indeed be surprising if they all used DNA as their genetic material; but even more surprising if they had all hit on the same code. The universality of the code is easy to understand if every species is descended from a common ancestor. Whatever code was used by the common ancestor would, through evolution, be retained. It would be retained because any change in it would be disastrous. A single change would cause all the proteins of the body, perfected over millions of years, to be built wrongly; no such body could live. It would be like trying to communicate, but having swapped letters around in words; if you change every 'a' for an 'x', for example, and tried talking to people, they would not make much sense of it. Thus we expect the genetic code to be universal if all species have originated from a single ancestor. It is another case of the homological argument for evolution. The homological argument favours evolution against both alternatives: it counts against transformism as well as separate creation.

We now come to the final argument for evolution: the fossil record. The fossil record offers two candidate arguments for evolution. One is the direct observation of evolutionary change over geological time. Because geological time lasts longer than the life of any single human being, we might hope that the fossil record would show more extensive evolutionary change than those cases of directly observed evolution that we have dealt with. The second kind of geological argument steps back from observations of single evolutionary lineages, to consider the pattern of the fossil record as a whole. This leads to the argument from what Darwin called (in a chapter title) 'the geological succession of organic beings'. Let us consider the two in turn.

The fossil record of evolutionary change within single evolutionary lineages is very poor. If evolution is true, species originate through changes of ancestral species: one might expect to be able to see this in the fossil record. In fact it can rarely be seen. In 1859 Darwin could not cite a single example. He attributed the absence of examples to the incompleteness of the fossil record. Thus the chapter of *On the Origin of Species* in which he considers this first geological argument is entitled 'On the imperfections of the geological record'. There are now some cases in which evolutionary change can be seen in the fossil record. A few dozen could be listed. But the most striking thing about them is their rarity. This being so, the first geological argument cannot provide a strong argument for evolution. With the accumulation of evidence it may become a powerful argument; but at present it is not. Nor, of course, is the rarity of observable evolution in the fossil record an argument against evolution. That rarity is exactly what an evolutionist would expect if the fossil record contained many gaps: and it is known that the fossil record is very incomplete. We shall return to that in Chapter 9.

The second geological argument is more successful. For this argument we retreat from the evolutionary change of single lineages, to look instead at the distribution of the main animal groups in time. Take the vertebrates as an example. Fish first appear in the fossil record before amphibians, amphibians appear before reptiles, reptiles appear before mammals, with a clear sequence of progressively more mammal-like reptiles, in the right order, in between; the first mammals appear before the smaller sub-groups of mammals, such as apes; humans appear only about a million years ago. This sequence is exactly what the theory of evolution predicts. In order for a mammal to evolve from a fish it would have to go through amphibian, then reptilian, and then mammal-like reptilian stages; the evolutionist therefore expects these groups to appear in the fossil record in the order they do. Conversely, he would be very worried if they appeared in some other order. Creationist critics of evolution have therefore made a great song and dance about purported fossil human footprints from the Cretaceous, contemporary with the dinosaurs. If such footprints really did exist, they would seriously challenge evolution. The evolutionary descent of humans fits in well with the fossil record if humans originated a few million years ago. Before that there is a good sequence of general ancestral forms: there are anthropoid apes, and then, moving backwards in time, more generalized primate forms, more generalized mammals, and so on. The fossil record provides no such sequence of possible ancestors for a human living in the Cretaceous. A Cretaceous human would exist in evolutionary isolation, without any obvious fossils connecting it with other vertebrates of that time. If humans evolved, they must have evolved from ancestors, and there ought to be at least possible ancestors in the fossil record near to (or just before) humans in time. In the Cretaceous there are not.

In fact the supposed Cretaceous human footprints are almost certainly not human footprints at all. But if a discovery of that kind were made it would worry the evolutionist. Thus there is an argument for evolution in the fact that these discoveries are not made. The pattern of the geological succession, as a whole, fits evolution very well.

It does not fit the theory of separate creation. If fish, amphibians, reptiles, mammal-like reptiles, and mammals had been created separately, it would be too great a coincidence that they should appear in the fossil record in exactly the order predicted by evolution. If mammals and fish had separate but contemporary origins, why are no mammals at all found in the fossil record as early as fish? There is one possible reason. Something like the theory of separate creation, as I have said, was held at one time by Charles Lyell. Lyell was a geologist, well aware of the pattern of the geological succession. He tried to reconcile it with separate creation by arguing that the groups that were common at a particular time were those favoured by the prevailing environmental conditions. Changes in which groups were common (he supposed) were caused by changes in the environment. Thus amphibians came after fish because the environment so changed as to enable amphibians to become relatively more abundant, and therefore relatively more likely to leave a fossil record.

Lyell's explanation of the geological succession might stand up if the geological succession were the only argument for evolution. It is a forced argument, but difficult to refute decisively. The main reason for supposing that Lyell was wrong (and it is the reason why he himself changed his mind in the 1860s) is that we have abundant other reasons for supposing that evolution, rather than separate creation, is true. Once we accept evolution we can abandon Lyell's forced argument more confidently. The geological succession fits the theory of evolution.

We have now completed a summary of the main arguments for evolution. The combination of observations of evolution on the small scale, with the principle of uniformitarianism, the nature of classification, the argument from homologies such as the universality of the genetic code, and the geological succession of organic beings, if not the evidence of observed evolution in fossils, all make up a convincing case. We have only been through the main classes of evidence: the number of examples could be multiplied by a large factor. We could also have considered another powerful argument for evolution. No sensible alternative is known. Our two alternatives, separate creation and transformism, are not really coherent. They merely suppose that species are created somehow; but they fail to specify a mechanism. As we shall see, there is a mechanism to explain evolution. It is called natural selection, and is utterly inconsistent with separate creation, if not transformism. Natural selection created species by modifying existing ones, not by creating them from nothing. The absence of any coherent alternative to natural selection as a mechanism of creating species is by itself a powerful reason for accepting evolution.

Our first problem of evolution, I believe, is solved. The accumulation of facts and arguments on the side of evolution is so great that it can no longer be considered an open question. It is best that our beliefs should be rationally based: it is well worth knowing what the case for evolution is. But once the case has been examined, it is not really possible for anyone (who is not a fanatic) to doubt what the conclusion must be.

2 The Nature of Heredity

With the fact of evolution established, the next problem is to explain why it takes place. What is the mechanism of evolution? What is its cause? The first possible source of an answer is heredity. New forms might spontaneously arise in the process of reproduction, and evolution be the automatic consequence of inheritance. For evolution to result, the new forms would have to arise in a fairly consistent direction. But common sense and everyday observation do not suggest that they do. We know that cows do usually reproduce cows. There are, however, two other possibilities, which might escape everyday observation. One is that the reproduction of new species from cows might take place in many insensibly small stages rather than in one obvious stage: from an initially cow-like state, small changes might gradually accumulate, to result in the evolution of a new species. The other possibility is that, although cows do not usually reproduce new species, they might do so on very rare occasions; a whole new species might be formed by a single hereditary alteration.

Of course, heredity may not itself produce evolution. Some other process may be responsible. We must look to the facts of heredity to settle the matter. If the facts of heredity can account for evolution, the problem is solved. And even if they cannot, they will still be important as we go on to consider other possible mechanisms of evolution, for any other theory of evolution will at least have to be consistent with the facts of heredity.

Let me remark at the outset that the problem has been solved. The relevant facts are just that, facts, and they have to be accepted as such. Heredity is of a kind that is usually called (after its discoverer) Mendelian. I shall illustrate the nature of

Mendelian heredity by one of Gregor Mendel's own experiments, and then consider its implications for the mechanism of evolution.

Mendel's most important experiments were conducted with pea plants. He divided his peas into classes defined by different, paired traits, short and tall plants for example, and then worked out how they were inherited. He first obtained pure breeding lines of the classes of pea. This means that an individual of the line, when crossed with another individual of the same line, always breeds true; in a pure line of short pea plants, for example, when one short plant is crossed to another, it always reproduces only short plants. Mendel then crossed peas from a pure tall line with peas from a pure short line, and studied their offspring. The offspring of this cross are all tall: there are no short and no inter-mediate-sized offspring. So far so good, but the next stage of the experiment was more revealing. He took the tall individuals pro-duced by the cross between lines, and crossed them together. These tall plants did not breed true. The offspring in the second generation were both tall and short, in the approximate ratio of three tall plants for every short one.

Mendel explained his results as follows (Figure 2). Suppose that each pea has two factors (let us call them by their modern name, genes) controlling the trait. The two relevant genes in any one individual of one of the pure parental lines are the same. Let us symbolize the pair of genes (called a genotype) of the tall line as TT, and of the short line as tt. Now, when an individual repro-duces it makes gametes, which are called pollen and ovules in plants (sperms and eggs in animals). Each gamete contains only one of the pair of genes. The gametes of a tall plant (TT) contain one of its two T genes; those of one of the initial short plants con-tain one t gene. Reproduction takes place by the fusion of the gametes of two individuals. In Mendel's first cross, all the new individuals were reproduced by the fusion of one T gene from the tall parent and one t gene from the short parent. All the offspring thus have the genotype Tt. They were all (as we have seen) tall. This Mendel explained by the 'dominance' of the T gene over the t gene. (Dominance means that the trait of the dominant gene is expressed when it is in combination with its complementary kind of gene, which is called recessive.)

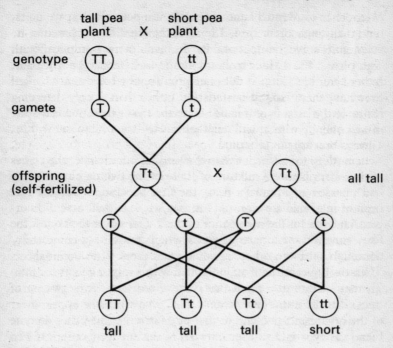

Fig. 2. A simple Mendelian cross.
Two types of pea plant, tall (genotype *TT*) and short (*tt*) are crossed. The offspring are all tall, but because they are all heterozygotes (*Tt*), when self-fertilized they reproduce tall and short plants in the ratio 3 to 1 (1 *TT* : 2 *Tt* : 1 *tt*).

We now know all we need to explain the second generation. It was formed from crosses of two *Tt* parents. Each parent produces *T* gametes and *t* gametes in equal proportions. The gametes of the two parents fuse: half the *T* gametes of one parent fuse with *T* gametes from the other parent and half with *t* gametes; and similarly half its *t* gametes fuse with the other parent's *T* and half with its *t*. What proportions of genotypes does that give? There is one way of forming *TT* and one of forming *tt*; but there are two ways of forming *Tt*. The total proportions therefore are 1 *TT* : 2 *Tt* : 1 *tt*. The *Tt* peas are tall, because *T* is dominant. The ratio of tall plants to short will be 3 : 1, as they are.

Many tests of Mendel's interpretation are possible, but we need not go through them here. Let us accept that his explanation is valid and move on to consider its evolutionary implications. There are, I think, four main implications: heredity is particulate rather than blending; it does not produce any consistent change between generations; it is statistical rather than simply deterministic; and what a parent hands on to the next generation is determined only by what it had itself inherited—traits acquired within a generation are not inherited.

According to the hypothesis of blending inheritance, the traits of the offspring are a mixture of those of the two parents. If size had blended in Mendel's peas, the first generation would have been of intermediate size, not (as they were) all tall. Size did not blend because of the dominance of the T genes over the t ones. In fact, however, with pairs of genes, one is not always completely dominant over the other; in some cases there is no dominance. Then the appearance of an individual with a mixed genotype (like Tt) may be intermediate between the appearance of the two pure lines. But the important point is that, even when the appearance of the organism is a blend of that of its parents, the genes do not blend. They would still separate out in the next generation. If Tt, for example, had been of intermediate size, the ratios of TT, Tt, and tt would still have been 1 : 2 : 1 in the next generation: there is no *genetic* blending. Genetic blending would mean that when a T joined a t, it would mix to form some intermediate kind of gene (call it t_1) which produced an intermediate-sized plant. That does not happen. The T and t do not blend. They are particulate genes.

What difference does it make to evolution that heredity is particulate rather than blending? Under blending inheritance, variants are gradually lost as they all blend into one; but with particulate inheritance the variants are conserved. If two genes blended, one kind of gene would exist where there were two kinds before. If that process were then continued for long enough, there would soon be only one kind of gene in the whole population.

Consider what happens, under blending inheritance, when a new variant appears in the population. Suppose that only one copy of the new variant appears, in a large population. We can call the new variant m_1; all the rest of the population possesses another gene, which we can call m. The gene might (for instance) control coloration: m might cause green colour, m_1 white. Now suppose that (by some mechanism that we have not specified) m_1 starts to increase in frequency in the population from generation to generation. What will happen? In the first generation, the single m_1 will mate with an m individual, because all the other members of the population are m; m and m_1 will blend, to produce some new kind of gene m_2, which in turn causes its bearers to be a pale green blend of its parental colours. m_1 has now been lost. The population now consists mainly of m individuals, with a few m_2 individuals. In the next generation, the m_2-bearing individuals will practically all mate with m individuals (because m_2 are still in a tiny minority), to produce another kind of gene m_3, which produces a colour between pale green and green. This process need not continue for long before the effect of the new variant has been swamped out by the ancestral, majority form. The frequency of the variant could not increase much in the population before it had ceased to exist. From a single new variant, a population could not become all white. In order for the population to become all white, the m_1 gene would have to arise many times in succession; single variants could not have much evolutionary effect.

Under particulate inheritance, the story is not the same. Now the m_1 gene is not lost after the first generation. Suppose that it is dominant. mm_1 individuals are then white. Suppose also, again, that whiteness has a tendency to increase in frequency over the generations. The important point is that the m_1 gene will be passed on to the next generation. It is conserved. In theory it could increase in frequency until m had been eliminated, and m_1 was the only gene; the whole population would then be made up of white individuals. The m_1 gene would not need to arise repeatedly in order for the population to evolve from the white to the green state. A whole population can be converted from a single, or a very few, original new hereditary variants. Such is the importance of particulate inheritance for the theory of evolution.

The second evolutionary implication of Mendelian heredity is that the process of heredity alone does not produce directional change over time. At the start of this chapter we observed that inheritance alone might possibly produce evolution. That possibility can now be exploded by the facts of Mendelism. If we return to the original Mendelian experiment and count the frequencies of the different genes in successive generations, we can see that they are constant. In the parental generation there are two *T* genes in the tall parent, and two *t* in the short parents; there are equal numbers of the two kinds of parents, which gives equal proportions of *T* and *t*. In the second generation, all individuals are *Tt*; again the proportions are equal. In the third generation there are *TT*, *Tt*, and *tt* in the proportions 1 : 2 : 1, which again gives equal gene proportions. The pure process of Mendelian heredity does not produce any evolutionary change at all: the population stays the same. In the experiment, although the gene proportions stay the same, the proportions of the three different genotypes do not. In the first generation there are equal proportions of *TT* and *tt*, in the second they are all *Tt*, and in the third there are 1 *TT* : 2 *Tt* : 1 *tt*. But in fact this inconstancy is only due to the artificial starting point. If the members of the population were left to breed among themselves, it would soon settle down with constant proportions of genotypes as well as constant proportions of genes. The constant genotype proportions can be discovered mathematically, and are called the Hardy–Weinberg equilibrium. Whether we consider genes or genotypes, the population is constant. Heredity alone does not produce evolution.

Although the ratio of tall to short plants in the final generation of the Mendelian experiment was three to one, this is a statistical average. The exact ratio in Mendel's original experiment was 787 tall to 277 short (2.84 : 1), and it is usual in every such experiment for the ratios to be nearly, rather than exactly, what the Mendelian theory predicts. The reason is that the production of gametes and (more importantly) the combination of gametes to form new organisms are statistical processes.

When an organism such as a pea plant produces gametes, a single cell temporarily doubles its normal complement of two copies of each kind of gene up to four; it then divides twice to produce gametic cells which contain one copy of every gene. The male gametes (pollen) are produced in exactly the ratio of the plant's genotype: if the pea is *Tt* it produces exactly one *T* pollen for each *t* pollen. The production of female gametes is slightly different. For every ovule that is produced, three cells are killed. Only one of the products of the possible four becomes an ovule. In the male, therefore, the ratios of genes in the gametes of an individual is exactly deterministic; but in the female there is a slight random element at this stage. Three out of four gene copies are lost, and the one that survives is randomly chosen from the initial four copies.

The main statistical element enters at the next stage. When the gametes combine to form the next generation, only a tiny proportion of the total (so to speak) 'pool' of gametes is successful. Only a few of all the gametes actually manage to combine with another gamete, and grow into a new plant. Any pea plant produces millions of pollen grains, but only a few of them develop. Because the successful gametes are chosen more or less at random from the large pool of gametes, the ratios of genes in the next generation will be approximately what they were in the one before, but not exactly. They will be a statistical average.

It is worth spelling out exactly what random means here. Suppose that T and t genes are in equal proportions in the total pool of gametes. Now consider the first fertilization. Suppose that one T pollen fuses with one T ovule, to make a TT pea. The proportions of T and t in the next generation are (temporarily) one to zero. What random means is that, despite this temporary good fortune of the T gene, there will be no compensating good fortune for the t gene. The chance that the next gene sampled from the pool to build a new pea is a t remains, as before, 50 per cent. It is like tossing a coin. If three heads are tossed in a row, that does not make it any more probable that the next toss will be a tail. The chances remain 50 per cent. The chance that a gene will be sampled is almost independent of its previous good or bad fortune; its chance is always equal to its proportion in the gamete pool. That is the meaning of random sampling.

It can have important evolutionary consequences. Although Mendelian heredity cannot produce consistently directed evolutionary change, it can produce random change. The frequencies of genes in a Mendelian population will drift around; it is even possible that one gene might drift to a proportion of one (in other words, become established in the population). The random drift has been mathematically modelled, and its potential evolutionary consequences are known. Its real importance in evolution is a more difficult problem, as (in Chapter 5) we shall see.

The final, and most important, implication of Mendelian heredity is that it does not allow the inheritance of acquired characters. The inheritance of acquired characters is, historically, the main alternative to natural selection as a mechanism of evolution. It is often called Lamarckian inheritance. It is a possible mechanism by which heredity alone could produce evolution. The idea, explained in terms of the familiar example of the blacksmith's arm, is this. A man, to start with, is born with a genetic constitution giving him a certain degree of muscularity. If he then exercises his arms, by hammering on horses' hooves, he would grow more muscular. We know that for a fact. The question is what his children are going to turn out like. If acquired characters are inherited, they should turn out stronger (to begin with) than their father before he took up being a blacksmith. If acquired characters are not inherited, the acquired strength of the blacksmith will make no difference to the genes that his offspring inherit from him.

If the inheritance of acquired characters took place, it could be the mechanism of evolution. We know that the efforts of individuals during their lives produce changes. If these were inherited by the next generation, evolution would result. It is a valid theory of evolution in the sense that if its premise (the inheritance of acquired characters) were true, its conclusion would follow. It would still be open to question whether it could account for all known evolution; but at least it could explain some.

In fact acquired characters are not inherited. The blacksmith's arm is not inherited by his children. Let me repeat the point with an imaginary Mendelian pea experiment. The height of a pea plant could be altered by the nutritiousness of the soil it was grown in, or simply by cutting. If Mendel had cut some of his tall plants down to the size of his short ones, the ratios of tall and short in the next generation would have been exactly the same as if he had not. Changes acquired during the lifetime of an individual do not affect its hereditary constitution: acquired characters are not inherited. The inheritance of acquired characters is factually ruled out as the mechanism of evolution. We shall come later to a principled objection: we have here confined ourselves to factual ones.

The fact that acquired characters are not inherited can be expressed in another way. Call that part of the organism concerned with reproduction the germ line and all the rest (which dies when the organism dies) the soma. The non-inheritance of acquired characters is then due to the fact that heritable information cannot pass from the soma to the germ line. The germ line and soma are separate in evolution. This doctrine of the independence of the germ line was first most forcefully expressed by the German biologist August Weismann at the end of the nineteenth century; it is often called Weismannism. Weismannism rules out the possibility of the inheritance of acquired characters.

Not all organisms have Mendelian inheritance, but all have Weismannist inheritance. There are some organisms (particularly micro-organisms) that do not have two copies of each gene and do not produce gametes by a Mendelian reduction division of cells. But in all organisms there is a separation of germ and soma lines: in no organisms are acquired somatic changes inherited. Weismannism is a more general doctrine than Mendelism, which it includes as a special case. The doctrine of Weismannism is also valuable because it clearly identifies the crucial fact of inheritance, that the heritable properties of an organism, which are contained in its germ line, are not affected by the rest of the body.

That concludes the list of the four main evolutionary implications of Mendelian heredity. Before we move on, there is one remaining question to ask about heredity. What about the appearance of new, heritable traits? We have considered so far the inheritance of traits that already exist in the population, such as tallness in peas. But what about traits that do not already exist? They must be important in evolution. Evolution is not confined to the alteration of proportions of pre-existing types; fundamentally new traits sometimes arise.

New heritable traits can arise by two main mechanisms. One is called mutation, the other recombination. Mutations are physical changes in genes, which alter the gene's effect. If a gene G caused the production of a particular chemical, it might mutate to a new gene G_1 which produced a different chemical. Mutations are inherited by the offspring of the individual in which the mutation first appeared. They can therefore be the origin of evolutionary change. Genes mutate spontaneously, but at a low rate; typical rates of mutation are about once per million generations. The rate can be speeded up by certain treatments, such as some chemicals (e.g. mustard gas), X-rays, and the detonation of nuclear bombs.

Recombination produces novelty by recombining different, previously existing Mendelian genes. The Mendelian experiment that we considered concerned only one trait, size. But size is not the only property of a pea plant. There are hundreds of others— colour, resistance to cold, leaf shape. The other traits are also controlled by Mendelian genes. When the whole set of genes is passed on to the next generation, different genes may either be inherited independently, or they may be inherited as a unit. Genes are inherited together as a unit when they are (as it is called) linked.

Whether or not different genes are inherited independently depends on whether they are on the same chromosome. The chromosomes are the molecular structures that carry the genes: as chromosomes are passed from the parent into its gametes, the hereditary information is carried on them. (Chromosomes are large enough to be seen with a light microscope.) An individual contains more than one chromosome, although the exact number differs between species; humans, for example, possess 48 chromosomes; peas possess 14. If the genes controlling two different traits (say size and colour) are on different chromosomes, they will be inherited independently. But if two traits are on the same chromosome they tend to be inherited as a unit.

Recombination produces new kinds of organism by breaking up linked sets of genes. By a mechanism called crossing-over, which can be seen in a microscope, genes are recombined between pairs of chromosomes. This can generate new combinations of genes. They may not be inherited for long because further recombination may in turn break up the new combinations, but it can still produce new kinds of organisms. Recombination may be especially important in one particular evolutionary circumstance.

If two mutations arise in two different genes of a chromosome, at about the same time, the two will probably initially be carried in different individuals. Without recombination, the two mutations might never co-exist in the same physical chromosome: one of them would have to arise a second time, in the progeny of the other mutant. Recombination however can quickly put them together. If the two mutations have superior effects when together rather than when they are separate, this effect of recombination would speed up the rate of evolution.

We can now return to the original problem, of whether heredity alone can produce evolution. Because evolutionary innovations result from mutation and recombination, we should rephrase the question to ask whether mutation and recombination produce directed or undirected change. The answer is that, like pure Mendelian inheritance, they too are undirected. They do not consistently produce changes in any particular direction. Mutations affecting size are just as likely to produce taller organisms as shorter ones. Various theories of evolution by 'directed variation' have been proposed, but we must rule them out. There is no evidence for directed variation in mutation, in recombination, or in the process of Mendelian inheritance. Whatever the internal plausibility of these theories, they are in fact wrong. Neither the inheritance of acquired characters, nor any other theory of directed hereditary change (or directed mutation), is the mechanism of evolution.

The facts of inheritance, from mutation, recombination, and Mendelian heredity, could only account for randomly directed evolution. Because there is direction in evolution, we now need some other mechanism to account for it.

3 The Mechanism of Evolution

We have discussed so far two requirements of a valid theory of evolution: it must explain why evolution takes place and it must fit the facts of heredity. There is one further requirement. The theory must explain why organisms are well designed for life. The traits of organisms encoded by Mendelian genes are not just any old traits, and the changes of evolution are not any old changes. The traits of organisms are well designed; they are (as we say) adaptations.

An example may make the meaning of adaptation clear. The appearance of many animals makes them difficult to detect; they are camouflaged. Coloration, structure, and behaviour may all contribute. The coloration of many moths, for instance, resembles the tree bark on which they rest; the structure of leaf insects resembles a leaf. Behavioural adaptation is also necessary, for a camouflaged animal must be able to recognize and imitate the bit of the environment to which it is adapted. A leaf insect must settle on the branch of a tree—it would not be camouflaged on the trunk—and, like a leaf, it should sway gently in the breeze.

Camouflage is an adaptation. It makes the camouflaged animal less likely to be eaten by a predator. The camouflaged animal would survive better than a similar, but uncamouflaged, animal. Adaptation means good design for life. To understand how any particular property of an organism is adapted, it is necessary to think how it enhances its bearer's chances of survival and reproduction. For camouflage this is quite easy. Camouflage makes it more difficult for predators to see the camouflaged prey, which is therefore eaten less. That is the argument that allows us to call camouflage an adaptation; without it we could not say how camouflage was adaptive, or even whether it was an adaptation at all.

The problem of the mechanism of evolution is to find a theory that can explain evolution, that can explain adaptation, and that fits the facts of heredity. Only one theory is known that passes all three tests: the theory of natural selection. It is the work of this chapter to explain natural selection and to show that it can indeed account for all of the facts of evolution and adaptation. The absence of an alternative, together with the fact that no known properties of organisms are inconsistent with natural selection, means that this problem of evolution, like the previous two, is effectively solved. Not everyone, however, would agree.

To explain natural selection, we can stay with the case of camouflage. It supplies one of the classic pieces of work on natural selection, that of H. B. D. Kettlewell on industrial melanism in the peppered moth *Biston betularia* in Great Britain. This moth has two types, a dark melanic type and a lighter peppered type. The difference is controlled by Mendelian genes, although not by a single gene, as was the case for tall and short pea plants. The facts, considerably simplified, are these. Before the Industrial Revolution the peppered type was much the commoner of the two. Then in the early and mid-nineteenth century, in industrial areas, the melanic type increased in frequency to become the more abundant of the two; in non-industrial areas the peppered type remained the commoner. As industrial activity decreased in some areas during the twentieth century, the peppered type became common again.

Such are the facts. Now for the explanation. The soot discharged by great factories kills the lichen that grow on tree trunks, leaving the tree trunks bare and dark. The peppered type is camouflaged on a lichen-covered trunk, but not on a bare lichen-less trunk; the melanic type is camouflaged on the bare lichen-less trunks, but stands out on the lichen-covered, normal trunks. The moths are eaten by birds, which hunt for their prey visually. That is enough to explain the facts. During the Industrial Revolution, the background on which the moths settle changed colour. It changed from a light peppered colour to black. Where the peppered type had previously been camouflaged, it now became conspicuous: it was more easily seen by birds, and was eaten more. Where the melanic type was previously conspicuous, it now became camouflaged, and was eaten less. The change in the relative frequencies of the two types was caused by bird predation against a changing background.

Kettlewell checked his interpretation by experiment. He placed melanic and peppered types on tree trunks in industrial and in non-industrial areas; from a hide, he measured the rate at which the two kinds were taken by birds. The results fitted the theory. The birds behaved as it demanded. The melanic type was taken more in the non-industrial area, the peppered type in the industrial area.

The true causes of the change in the frequencies of peppered and melanic types of *Biston betularia* are known to be more complex than that simple summary. But the summary will serve to illustrate natural selection. The type that survived better, in one area, increased in frequency: there was an evolutionary change, towards the better-adapted type, in the moth population.

We have seen natural selection in an example. Let us now consider it in the abstract. What are the factors needed in order for evolution to result? The first is that the difference between types must be heritable. Evolution would be impossible otherwise. If the difference were not heritable, the offspring of the two types would both contain the same frequencies of melanic and peppered types; and then even if the melanic type survived better, and left more offspring, evolution would not take place towards the melanic type. Differential survival, although it cannot by itself produce evolution, is another requirement. In order for the melanic type to increase in frequency it had to survive better. But differential survival only matters because it usually results in differential reproduction. The melanic type actually increased in frequency in industrial areas because (being more likely to survive to reproduce) it contributed relatively more offspring to the next generation than did the peppered types.

Natural selection can also, in theory, work on differential reproduction without differential survival. If the two types survived equally well, but one laid more eggs on average than the other, then there would be an evolutionary increase in the frequency of the more fecund type even though the chance of survival of the two was the same.

We have now defined the abstract conditions for evolution by natural selection. The different types must be genetically different and they must reproduce at different rates; there must then automatically be an evolutionary increase in the frequency of the type that reproduces more. It is inevitable. If the premises are met, the conclusion must follow.

It is one thing to show that natural selection works in the case of camouflage. It is another to extend the principle to all the other traits of organisms. But Darwin provided a general argument. It is his famous Malthusian argument. Organisms produce more offspring than can survive: most of them die before maturity. The result is a perpetual struggle for existence. Any heritable improvement in any trait will therefore increase in frequency in the population. Natural selection is constantly at work on all the properties of an organism. Camouflage is not an exception.

Now that we have seen what natural selection is, we can ask whether it meets the three requirements to explain evolution, explain adaptation, and fit the facts of heredity. The example showed that it can, but let us consider how. It explains adaptation almost automatically. Forms that are better designed for life in their environments will tend to leave more offspring. By natural selection, they will come to predominate over less well designed forms.

The explanation is so automatic that some critics have suspected it is merely verbal. They have sniffed a tautology. Indeed, Darwin's argument has been accompanied, almost throughout its history, by the criticism that it is circular. The Bishop of Carlisle (I think) stated it first in 1890, but it has become especially popular recently. Natural selection is often summarized as 'the survival of the fittest'. (The phrase is Herbert Spencer's, not Darwin's. Darwin never liked it, although not because it made his argument sound circular.) The criticism is this. Survival just means staying alive; but what about 'the fittest'? That too, in the end, only seems to mean those that survive. 'The survival of the fittest' can then be translated as the survival of those that survive, which is clearly a tautology. As Sir Karl Popper has remarked, 'there is hardly any possibility of testing a theory as feeble as this'.

If the criticism is valid, Darwin's theory would be in peril. The interest of natural selection is that it purports to explain the traits of organisms. But if it is circular it cannot be explanatory. Circular arguments do not explain anything. If the only criterion of an adaptation is survival, natural selection *means* adaptation rather than explains it. The Darwinian theory therefore must possess a criterion of an adaptation independent of whether natural selection favours the trait. Fittest must mean more than just survival.

Let us reconsider the camouflage of *Biston betularia*, to see whether adaptation in this case means anything more than mere survival. If the theory of natural selection were circular it would merely say that the type that survived better increased in frequency in evolution. But is that all it says? No, it is not. The important part has been omitted: it is so obvious in this case that it might be overlooked by a hasty critic. The missing part is the explanation of why one type survives better: camouflage. Camouflage matters because peppered moths are killed by visually hunting birds. On a lichen-less trunk, the melanic type is less easy to see than the peppered type. The melanic type does increase in frequency where it survives best: but the explanation of this fact is that the melanic type is better camouflaged, and less subject to avian predation, in polluted woods.

The arguments concerning camouflage and predation provide the criterion of adaptation. They are independent of survival. They are also testable. We can test, by observation, whether melanic moths are better camouflaged in polluted areas. Human vision may differ from bird vision, but we can test for that too and (if necessary) make allowance. Measurements of which trait survives best in an environment are not the criterion of adaptation: the criterion comes from an argument of design, which must explain how the trait is designed for life in its natural environment, and whose assumptions have been tested as thoroughly as possible. The best-designed form should (if the argument is correct) also survive best. But the measurement of survival rates is a laborious task, rarely performed in practice. More often the biologist remains content with the argument of design. That argument alone provides the criterion, independent of survival, of the 'fittest' in that phrase 'the survival of the fittest'. The theory of natural selection that the Bishop of Carlisle and Sir Karl Popper thought tautologous was an incomplete version of the theory. When its original parts are restored, the circular argument becomes a scientific theory.

So natural selection passes the first test: it explains adaptation. But what about evolution? It succeeds here too, for it will cause evolution when the environment changes. The evolution of the moth population was driven by a change in the colour of its background environment. In this case the relevant environmental variable is fairly obvious. But the 'environment' will often be a more subtle property than background colour. It may be any property of the inanimate world in which the organism lives, or of the living forms that it competes with, of its own or other species. A predator is a part of the environment of its prey: a change in a predator that makes it better at finding prey will be experienced, by the prey species, as a change in the environment. The change may cause the evolution of some new counter-adaptation to foil the predator, or (failing that) it may drive the prey species extinct. A change in the courtship demands of a female will be experienced, by the male of the species, as an environmental change, which demands the evolution of new courting behaviour.

Finally, natural selection fits the Mendelian facts. We have seen that, within heredity, there is no directing process that could cause evolution. There is the potential for random drift, but not for directed change. This is exactly what natural selection requires. Natural selection itself acts as a directing process, which drives evolution towards adapted states. From heredity, it requires no more than raw material. Mendelism provides that. Raw material comes from recombination, mutation, and the inheritance of pre-existing genetic variants. Mendelian genes are particulate—they do not blend—which conserves the variation while natural selection operates on it.

So far we have considered only evolution on the small scale: changes in the relative frequencies of two pre-existing types, the peppered and melanic types, within one moth species. But natural selection can also produce a population of well-adapted moths from a new mutation. If the melanic type did not already exist in the industrial area, it might have arisen as a new mutation and exactly the same process could have carried it up to become the predominant type in the population. In order for the well-adapted type to be naturally selected it does have to appear to begin with by a chance mutation, but that is not very unlikely. Mutations will be appearing all the time, in all directions, some darker, some lighter, some with different patterns of peppering.

Mutation itself, it is important to realize, is not responsible for producing the population of adapted moths. Mutations are random, but adaptations are non-random states of nature. Mutation therefore cannot alone explain adaptation. Natural selection is needed, to select out those minority of mutants that happen to be adapted to the prevailing local environment. The selection, not the mutational, process produces adaptation. Chance is only needed to produce the random variation that selection works from. Darwinism emphatically is not a theory of evolution by chance. Unfortunately, some of its critics have supposed that it is. Starting with the distinguished astronomer Sir John Herschel, who after reading the *Origin* dismissed it as 'the law of higgledy piggledy', they have pointed out that Darwin's theory cannot possibly be right, because life is a highly non-random state of nature. The argument is correct, but misdirected: evolution cannot indeed be explained by chance, but natural selection does not try to do so.

Natural selection has passed all three tests. Its main alternatives are all theories of directed variation. The inheritance of acquired characters is the best known of them. How do these theories fare in our three tests? They can all explain evolution, but (as we saw in the previous chapter) they all fail on the facts of heredity. They could be rejected for that reason alone. But facts, in science, are often short-lived. Although no one has yet succeeded in demonstrating the inheritance of acquired characters (and not for want of trying, sometimes too hard) perhaps someone one day will succeed. It is therefore interesting to see whether the theory of the inheritance of acquired characters can survive the third test: can it, in principle, explain adaptation?

Richard Dawkins has asked this question. He has answered it too, in the negative. How does the inheritance of acquired characters explain adaptation? It is undoubtedly adaptive for a blacksmith to grow bigger muscles. If all the population followed the blacksmith's calling, they would presumably all grow bigger muscles. If that acquired adaptation were then inherited, the population would soon come to contain more muscular men, whose muscularity was adaptive. The inheritance of acquired characters does thus appear to explain adaptation. But when it is examined more closely, the appearance turns out to be deceptive. In truth, the theory takes the whole problem of adaptation for granted. That the blacksmith should make an adaptive response, growing larger muscles when larger muscles are needed, has been assumed; it has not been proved. But it needs proof. Why should a blacksmith's muscles grow larger when exercised? They might just as well grow smaller, because they are being used up. *In fact* they grow larger, but the fact itself is what needs to be explained. The extra growth is an adaptation, which the theory must explain, not merely take for granted.

To explain the adaptive response of the blacksmith's arm, the theory of the inheritance of acquired characters would have to fall back on some other theory that actually did explain adaptation. Natural selection is the only known theory that does. To grow bigger muscles when they are needed is an adaptive response. If that trait enabled the blacksmith's ancestors to reproduce more than competitors who lacked it, then it would have been favoured by natural selection. Even if acquired characters were inherited, therefore (which they are not), the true explanation of adaptation would have to come from the theory of natural selection. Without it the inheritance of acquired characters fails the third test.

All theories of 'directed' variation must suffer from the same defect. They all lack an explanation of how the directed variations manage to be adapted to the environment in which they must live. They must either fall back on natural selection to explain adaptation, or fail to explain it. In the former case, directed variation can be no more than an additional factor, and not an alternative, to natural selection; in the latter case, it must be rejected because it cannot explain the most striking feature of life, that living things are designed for living.

The same general kind of argument, although in a more specific form, has been turned against natural selection. Natural selection could undoubtedly have produced some kinds of adaptations, such as camouflage, but could it have produced them all? It has been argued that it could not. The particular kind of adaptation that (it has been said) natural selection in principle cannot produce may be exemplified by that highly complex structure, the eye. The eye is not only complex, but 'co-adapted' in the sense that the different parts making up the whole are closely adapted to each other. The shape of the lens, for instance, is adapted to the size of the eye. It is difficult to imagine how one part could be changed without appropriate changes in all the other parts that it co-operates with. Natural selection, however, can only change one part at a time, for the following reason. The chance of a single advantageous mutation is low enough; but the chance of simultaneous advantageous mutations, in the different parts of a complex organ, must be lower still. If the chance of one correct mutation is (say) less than one in a million, then the chance of ten correct ones would be impossibly small. For ten changes the chance will be one in 10^{-60}, which is far too low a probability for the event ever to have taken place. Natural selection can only work on mutations that actually have arisen, and advantageous mutations are only likely to arise one at a time. This being so, if there are complex organs that could only have arisen by exact changes in many different parts at the same time then they probably could not have evolved by natural selection. The critic of natural selection will claim that such organs exist; the Darwinian will reply that they do not. We have now defined the problem of co-adaptation.

The Darwinian theory has three solutions. The first, which we shall consider for the eye, is to argue that the co-adapted organ actually could have evolved in small stages, gradually improving at its constant function; let us call this piecemeal evolution. The second, which we shall consider for the evolution of flight, is to argue that the organ evolved in small stages, but that it changed its function during evolution. Feathers, for example, might initially have served in thermo-regulation, and only later have come to be used in flight. The third solution is symbiosis. In this case, the parts of a complex organ evolve separately, in different species, and are only put together later, when many of the parts have been separately perfected. In all three cases the Darwinian denies (as he must) that the complex co-adaptation arose in a single chance event.

I should have liked to use the origin of life as an example of piecemeal evolution. The origin of life is (next to the eye) the most commonly alleged instance of co-adaptation. The case against natural selection runs something like this. Even the simplest self-sufficient self-reproducing organisms, such as the simplest bacteria, contain many interacting parts. There is not only a complex hereditary molecule of DNA; there are also many (perhaps a minimum of 50) different proteins, a membrane, and other structures. They are all essential for the bacterium to live: if you took away any of them, it would die without reproducing. Natural selection could not then have built up bacteria from simpler forms of life. Without natural selection, all that the Darwinian is left with to explain the origin of the bacterium is chance. But the chance that molecules, combined at random, would form something as well designed as a bacterium is impossibly small.

For the pure nihilist, this is all very well. But for anyone who wants to understand the origin of life, it is something of a paradox. Natural selection is the only theory that we have to explain evolution; an explanation, if it is going to come from anywhere, will come from natural selection. If it really were true that no living thing could be simpler than a bacterium, then we really should have a problem. But no one has ever proved that simpler life forms could not exist. The Darwinian would try to explain the origin of life through a series of intermediate stages between a pre-biotic chemical stage and the bacterium. Such intermediate stages can be imagined. But merely imagining them does not serve any very useful purpose. What are required are chemical experiments on the possible life forms that could have arisen from a pre-biotic chemistry. Such experiments have been, and are being, conducted in great numbers; but still so little is known about the origin of life that it cannot support an instructive discussion of co-adaptation. The discussion would be excessively speculative. The origin of life is a case in which ignorance cuts both ways. If a Darwinian cannot prove that life did evolve from pre-biotic chemicals by natural selection, nor can a critic prove that it did not.

So for our example of the gradual, piecemeal evolution of a complex organ, let us return to the eye. Actually, the intermediate stages in the evolution of the eye are not known for sure; but some plausible intermediates do at least exist. They enable a relatively concrete discussion. It has often been declared by critics of Darwinism that so complex, so co-adapted an organ as the eye could not have been built in small stages by natural selection; to be advantageous it would have to exist as a whole; part of an eye would be useless. But when it is considered in detail it starts to appear more possible. Darwin gave two reasons for thinking that the eye evolved in small stages: that we can both imagine functional simple eyes, and that we can find them in living species.

The simplest kind of eye is a bowl-shaped invagination on the surface of the animal, with pigmented light-sensitive cells around the bowl. Leeches and flatworms possess this kind of eye. They cannot see much with it, but it does indicate the general direction of light and can sense the presence of any object that is so large or close that it blocks the outside opening of the bowl. It is easy to imagine that natural selection could favour such an eye. It is also easy to imagine how it could arise by a single chance mutation: the mutation only has to produce a light-sensitive pigment.

In the next stage, the bowl becomes larger and the hole (that opens to the outside) smaller. It is an improvement, because it makes the eye able to discriminate smaller objects. It increases the eye's resolution. This kind of pin-hole camera eye is rather rare in nature, but the mollusc *Nautilus* has one. The resolution of the eye increases as the pin-hole gets smaller, but there is the disadvantage that it lets in less light. The obvious next stage is to evolve a lens.

The simplest kind of lens is only a small change from the lensless pin-hole camera of *Nautilus*. A jelly, that fills the eye, extending from the transparent opening to the light-sensitive retina, can act as a lens. It is a simple and optically poor lens; it cannot form an image, but does allow the opening to the outside to be larger than in the pin-hole camera eye. It could therefore be advantageous: natural selection could favour it. Some types of worm, such as *Nereis*, have a jelly-filled eye. The next stage is to improve the material of the lens and to decrease its size. There can then be a gap between lens and retina, which will make room for an image to form.

We have now reached, by small steps, the best-engineered eyes in nature, those of the cephalopods and vertebrates. A few more improvements are needed to reach that final stage—special techniques to correct for close-up vision and refined optical aberrations—but we need not go into them. Enough has been said to show how even a complex, co-adapted organ could have evolved, by natural selection, in many small stages, without the need for an impossible coincidence of random mutations.

In the evolution of the eye, if the story above is correct, the function of the evolving organ remained constant: it was always an adaptation for seeing. In the evolution of other complex organs there may have been a change in function. The evolution of flight may provide an example. The case against natural selection would here run like this. If feathers were an adaptation for flight, they could not have evolved by natural selection until the bird could already fly. But in order for a bird to fly it needs a fairly well formed wing. The wing must be powerful and of the correct aerodynamic shape. Any stage intermediate in strength or design between a flightless and a flying form could not support flight, and could not be favoured. Natural selection, then, could not have driven evolution from a scaly, flightless to a feathered, flying form.

Or could it? The problem of strength is not difficult. Wings could not support powered flight without many other structural adaptations, but a feebler apparatus could support passive flight. An early stage of a wing might, for instance, have eased falls from trees. At the next stage the wings might be substantial enough to enable a longer period of gliding. Thus wings could have increased in strength, under natural selection, from weak beginnings to their modern powerful form. That is the same principle as we used for the eye. Feathers, however, illustrate a different principle. Feathers are adapted for flight, but that is not their only function. By trapping a layer of air next to the body surface, they also assist in thermo-regulation. Feathers may have evolved first to help small warm-bodied proto-birds retain their body heat. Only later did they assist in flight. Their function then changed, or at least became more complex.

While feathers have adapted for flight, they have kept their original function of thermo-regulation. A more extreme change would be for an organ, after a change of function, to lose its original function, in what A. G. Cairns-Smith has called an evolutionary takeover. The elephant's trunk, in the interpretation of D. M. S. Watson, may be an example. In ancestors of the modern elephant, which are known from fossils, the lower jawbone was extended far forwards, and used to scoop and excavate food from the ground. The upper lip would have extended forwards to meet the lower jaw; it would also have been mobile, to move food back into the mouth. The upper lip then became sufficiently manœuvrable to pick up and put food into the mouth without the support of the long lower jaw. The lower jaw was then lost, and the extended upper lip was left by itself as a trunk. It had evolved outwards to meet an ever extending lower jaw; but when that jaw was lost, the trunk had taken over for itself the whole function of feeding. The initial and intermediate stages can no longer be seen among modern forms, but they can be (after some interpretation) in the fossil record. Without that fossil evidence, which happens to be particularly good for elephants, the initial evolution of the elephant's trunk might have been difficult to explain.

The third Darwinian answer to the problem of complexity is evolution by symbiosis. Let us take as an example the evolution of the eukaryotic cell. In nature, there are two main kinds of cell. Simple organisms such as bacteria are of the cellular type called prokaryotic; more complex organisms, including all plants and animals, are built of eukaryotic cells (Figure 3). The most important difference between eukaryotic and prokaryotic cells is that eukaryotic cells have a nucleus. The nucleus is a separate compartment containing, within a membrane, the eukaryotic genetic material. The prokaryotic cell has no separate nucleus and the genetic material floats freely within the cell. There are other differences too. Most eukaryotic cells possess organelles called mitochondria; mitochondria are the cell's boiler houses, which

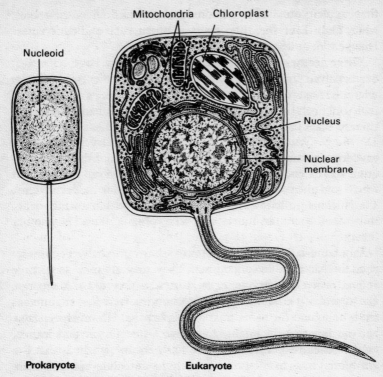

Fig. 3. Prokaryotic and eukaryotic cells.
The eukaryote has greater internal distinction, containing such organelles as mitochondria and chloroplasts. Some eukaryotic cells lack some of the organelles shown here: animals, for instance, lack chloroplasts.

supply the cell with energy. Within plant cells there are organelles called chloroplasts, which are the site of photosynthesis.

Prokaryotes evolved before eukaryotes. The earliest prokaryotic fossils are from almost the earliest rocks on the Earth, about 3,500 million years old. It is not known when eukaryotes first evolved. The earliest uncontroversial eukaryotic fossils are only about 700 million years old. All we can say is that the eukaryotic cell probably evolved from the prokaryotic cell between 3,500 and 700 million years ago. Now, eukaryotes are much more complex than prokaryotes. If evolution must proceed in small stages, where are the intermediates between prokaryotes and eukaryotes? Nowhere to be seen.

There are two main theories of how the eukaryotic cell might have evolved from the prokaryotic. One is the theory of internal differentiation, according to which the complexities of the eukaryotic cell evolved from the less complex parts of their prokaryotic ancestors; all the evolutionary stages would then have been internal changes inside the prokaryotic cell. If it is correct, there must have been a smooth series of evolutionary stages, like in the evolution of the eye, between the prokaryotes and eukaryotes, but which are not now preserved either in fossils or modern forms. The nucleus probably did evolve internally within a prokaryote. But for the mitochondria and chloroplasts there is another theory.

Mitchondria and chloroplasts may have originally been independent bacteria-like organisms. They may at some stage have entered other prokaryotic cells. Just why they did is a separate question, but perhaps the pre-mitochondria were just engulfed as food, or joined for some temporary purpose. However that may be, the partnership might then have lasted longer and longer, until it became permanent. The partnership (which is called a symbiosis) was advantageous to both the mitochondria, which are provided with food, and the host cell, which gains energy. Conversely, the chloroplast provides food, manufactured in photosynthesis, to the cell in which it lives, and obtains raw materials. After millions of years of evolutionary dependence on their host cells, mitochondria and chloroplasts have given up their means of independence. They retain only a few curious vestiges (if the symbiosis theory is correct) of their former lives.

The vestiges (if that is what they are) of former independence retained by mitochondria and chloroplasts are the main evidence that they originated as symbiotic partners of the cells they now inhabit. For instance, chloroplasts and mitochondria both possess some genetic material; and both look rather like modified bacteria. Moreover, the molecules made by their genes are more similar to their equivalents in free-living bacteria than to their equivalents made by the eukaryotic cell they occupy. Why should mitochondria make bacteria-like molecules if they were not once independent bacteria themselves?

The symbiotic theory of the origins of the mitochondria and chloroplast is not universally accepted. But we only need it to illustrate a principle. When a symbiotic innovation takes place during evolution, there can be a great increase in the complexity of life. This is true of symbiosis in general. In the case of the eukaryotic cell, the increase in complexity would be particularly large and of immense evolutionary importance. But if the symbiotic theory of eukaryotic origins is false, the principle still stands. There are many other examples of symbiosis: no biologists doubt that some symbiotic events have taken place in evolution. At the origin of each new symbiotic association, a new level of complexity would be created in a single event, without contradicting the theory of natural selection. The new level of complexity is created only by recombining previously existing complex organization, which in turn must have been built up in small stages.

Natural selection can therefore account for the evolution of the eye, of flight, and of the eukaryotic cell. All three organs at first appear impossible to build up in a series of small but advantageous stages. But in fact they probably were. I chose them as difficult tests for the theory of natural selection. If it can explain these, it can probably explain other cases as well. There are no known organs that natural selection definitely cannot explain.

In all these cases, including symbiosis, complex organs have been built up in small stages. Now that the principle is established we can use it more aggressively. Let us just watch it in action against the theory of macro-mutations. A macro-mutation is a very large mutation, one that produces a whole new organ, such as a liver or a heart, in a single mutational event. According to the Darwinian theory, macro-mutations are unimportant in evolution. The reason is that all the right changes needed to make a complex organ like a liver could not possibly all spontaneously arise at the same time. Mutational changes arise by chance changes in pre-existing parts; all the changes needed to make a liver would therefore have to arise by chance. That is not possible. The only way that an unlikely state of nature such as a liver could have evolved from chance changes, is for the changes to be spread out over a long time Then each change, provided that it is small, will have sufficient opportunity to arise by chance. That a light-sensitive pigment might arise in a cell by chance is not improbable. That a whole eye could so arise is impossible. That is why Darwinism excludes macro-mutations. Complex adaptations must have evolved by the natural selection of a large number of small mutations over a long period of time.

4 Natural Selection in Action

The Darwinian theory would explain the forms and diversity of the living world with a theory of variation and a theory of selection. To explain any particular trait in any particular species, the Darwinian asks what heritable variants of the trait are possible and which of them natural selection would favour in the circumstances of the species. The theory of variation should predict the range of variation; the theory of selection should predict which variants will be established.

The last twenty-five years have seen a great expansion in our understanding of natural selection. It has increased in depth, as the fundamentals of the process have been clarified; it has broadened in range, as it has been discovered how to apply it to more and more of the properties of organisms. In 1984, for example, we know much more about the influence of natural selection on social behaviour than we did in 1960.

But while the theory of selection has advanced, the theory of variation has not. The Darwinian therefore can only apply his sophisticated theory of selection with a primitive theory of variation. For a typical trait we do not know the range of possible variants, nor their relative frequencies. Of course the actual range of variation of a trait can be measured in nature; but this is only a minimum estimate of the range available for natural selection over evolutionary time, for new mutations can appear. The evolution of the sex ratio provides an example. In many species, including humans, the sex ratio is half males to half females, but it could imaginably be anything between zero and one. As it happens, we possess a highly advanced theory of the natural selection of the sex ratio; but about its variation we know very little. In the absence of knowledge we are forced to make an assumption. The theory has been applied in this case using the assumption that the sex ratio could vary between zero and one. We can then ask which sex ratio is favoured. The assumption here is that any possible variant can arise: it is reasonable; but it is only an assumption: it is not guaranteed by observation or theory.

In this chapter we shall consider how the Darwinian applies the theories of selection and variation to explain the forms of life. We shall not be concerned with particular traits *per se*, except to illustrate the general problem of analysis. We shall mainly be concerned with the more advanced part of Darwinism, the theory of selection: we shall consider the fundamentals of natural selection, which any hypothesis concerning a particular trait must satisfy; we shall then consider the general methods by which such a hypothesis can be tested. Only then shall we return to make mainly negative remarks about that most frustrating of Darwinian black sheep, the theory of variation.

How does natural selection act? What exact kinds of traits does it favour? These questions must obviously be answered before we can predict the traits of organisms. In a loose sense, natural selection favours traits that are good for the organisms concerned; but if we are to apply the theory we shall need a more precise statement than that. Otherwise we shall be faced with insoluble paradoxes in which different traits appear to be advantageous to different natural units, such as the group and the individual. Their advantages, for instance, conflict in the evolution of altruism. An altruistic act (in the biological sense of the word) is one that benefits the recipient at a cost to the altruist, benefit and cost being measured in terms of numbers of offspring produced. Altruism is by definition disadvantageous to the altruistic individual; but it could be advantageous to the group containing it, if the benefit to the recipient exceeds the cost to the altruist, for then the total reproduction of the group will be increased. We cannot predict whether altruistic behaviour should evolve unless we know whether natural selection favours the individual organism or the group. The whole problem is broader. The biological world can be classified into a series of increasingly inclusive levels: the gene, the chromosome, the entire genome, the cell, the organ, the organism, the family of kin, the group, the species, the genus, etc., up to the phylum, kingdom, and the entire biosphere. There can be conflicts between any of these levels. If we are to explain the traits of organisms correctly we shall need to know which level natural selection acts for the benefit of. In general terms, that level will be the one the frequency of whose different types natural selection most directly alters during evolution. The types that reproduce most will increase in frequency. They will be established by natural selection, and will be the traits that we observe in nature. The level at which natural selection acts is called the unit of selection. The argument to identify the unit of selection that we are about to consider is mainly due to George C. Williams and Richard Dawkins.

We cannot identify the unit of selection simply by looking for the level at which, during evolution, frequencies change. Frequencies change at all levels. In the evolution of *Biston betularia* for instance, not only the frequencies of different kinds of moths change; so too do the different kinds of moth genes, moth chromosomes, chemical pigments, as well as (for that matter) the kinds of moth species and even the ecosystems they inhabit. Their frequencies all change during evolution because they are all connected. If natural selection directly adjusted the frequency of moth genes, the frequency of moth chromosomes and moth organisms would automatically be adjusted as well, for chromosomes and organisms both contain genes; the same can be said *mutatis mutandis* of all other levels. We have a problem of cause and correlation: the question is which level (if any) is driving all the rest.

In fact the gene is the unit of selection. The evolutionary changes at all other levels are driven by the natural selection of genes. That, however, is to jump to the conclusion; our immediate concern should be its justification. Natural selection can only alter the frequency of something that is inherited from one generation to the next. Consider just two levels, the organism and the gene. Are they inherited? Genes are: if a new kind of gene arises, natural selection can alter its frequency. If the new gene reproduces faster than the old one its frequency will increase and *vice versa*. But now suppose that some new form of organism arose. Can natural selection alter its frequency? Only if the change is genetic. If the change is acquired, like the muscularity of a blacksmith's arm, it will not be inherited (p. 22) and its frequency will not be affected by natural selection. The arrow of causality points one way: a change in a gene causes a change in the organism that bears it, but not the other way round.

The non-inheritance of acquired characters narrows the field; but it is not enough to prove that the gene alone is the unit of selection. It only proves that the unit must be an instrument of heredity; but the chromosome and the genome are as much a part of heredity as is the gene. We must take the argument a stage further. The unit of selection must not merely be a part of the mechanism of inheritance, it must itself be inherited in identical form from generation to generation. It must be stable through evolutionary time. You can only alter the frequency of something if it stays the same while you are doing so. Now, genes do have this property of permanence; but chromosomes and genomes do not. The reason is meiotic recombination. An organism possesses a double set of chromosomes, and every generation genes are reshuffled within the chromosomal pairs during an event called meiosis. An offspring therefore does not inherit the exact chromosomes of its parent: chromosomes are not heritable. But genes are. Except for mutations, which are very rare, genes are copied exactly each generation.

The justification is complete. Only genes are sufficiently stable over evolutionary time for their frequency to be directly changed by natural selection. Natural populations, we should therefore predict, will contain well-adapted genes, genes that reproduce as numerously as possible in the circumstances. Any gene with increased powers of reproduction will be favoured. To understand why adaptations exist we should ask how they increase the reproduction of the genes that produce them.

Natural selection produces adaptations for the benefit of genes because the gene is the unit of selection. That however provides only a means of solution, not the solution itself, to the original problem. We wished to know whether the advantage of a group or of an organism would win in a conflict between them. The answer must be whichever is favoured by the natural selection of genes; but the argument we have considered so far does not tell us which one that is. Genes do not reproduce themselves in a vacuum. They exist in cells, in bodies, and sometimes in groups of bodies. They reproduce in the reproduction of these larger entities. We know that adaptations will exist that increase the reproduction of genes; what we must now ask is whether in general those adaptations will benefit cells, organisms, groups, or some other level.

As we ascend through the levels of the biological world, the degree of genetic independence changes. Consider two cases, the relation of cell and organism, and that of organism and group. By and large all the cells of an organism are genetically identical and the genes of all the cells are reproduced through a single cell line, the germ line (p. 23) which produces the sperms or eggs. The evolutionary fate of the genes in all the cells are coupled. The only method by which they can increase in frequency is by increasing the reproduction of the body that contains them. And that will increase the frequencies of all the genes of all the cells of that body by the same amount. One cannot increase independently of the other. There is no conflict between cell selection and organism selection. Now consider the organisms of a group. The genetic relation is completely changed. The organisms all differ genetically, and reproduce independently. A gene that makes its organismal bearer reproduce more than the other organisms will increase in frequency. For instance, in the example we started out from, of altruistic behaviour, genes for organismal selfishness will increase in frequency within a group of altruistic organisms. They must do, by definition. But a group of altruists will out-reproduce a group of selfish organisms. The genetic independence of organisms opens up the possibility of a conflict between organismal and group selection. But which will win? Will genes that confer organismal selfishness or altruism be established by natural selection?

The answer is decided by the relative rates of organismal and group selection. The trait will prevail in nature that is produced by the faster process. In the case of altruism and selfishness, organismal selfishness is favoured within a group by organismal selection; but groups of altruistic organisms go extinct less often, and reproduce more rapidly, than groups with more selfish members. (Group reproduction takes place when a new colony is set up by members of the 'parental' group.) Group selection favours altruism. Organismal selection favours selfishness. Group selection takes place over the time-scale of group extinction and group reproduction; organismal selection operates by organismal death and reproduction. Organismal selection therefore must be faster. It is logically impossible for a group to become extinct without the death of all its members; but organisms do die without group extinction. If a group of altruists ever did come into existence, organismal selection would rapidly convert the group to selfishness: the group would then be more likely to go extinct, but extinction in nature is uncommon relative to organismal death. If we look at species at any one time, the majority should show adaptations of organismal selfishness. Only if the organisms of a group were as tightly coupled genetically as the cells of a body should we expect adaptations for group benefit. If all the reproduction of a group were performed by one individual and all the members of the group were the offspring of a single founder, then all the members of the group might sacrifice themselves to assist that one individual. But groups in nature are not usually like that; group selection is not therefore expected to overrule organismal selection in the propagation of genes.

Natural selection fundamentally adjusts the frequencies of genes, and establishes those genes that produce such adaptations as enable them to out-reproduce other genes. The appropriate question to ask of the traits of an organism is 'would a gene for that trait reproduce more than that of any other (genetically possible) trait?' In nature, the natural selection of genes will usually result in adaptations that increase organismal reproduction. Within an organism there is genetic cohesion; a gene can only increase its reproduction by increasing that of all the other genes in the body. At higher levels, such as the group, there is genetic independence; a gene can increase its own reproduction independently of the other genes in the group. That adaptations should generally benefit organisms is only a predictable consequence of a more fundamental theory. Gene selection will produce adaptations to benefit the level below which there is genetic cohesion and above which there is genetic independence, whatever level that may be. In the exceptional cases in which the crucial level is not the organism, we should no longer expect adaptations to benefit the organism. The exceptions might prove the rule; but we shall not examine them here.

We have now established the fundamental conditions that any hypothesis about adaptation must satisfy. But for any particular trait there can be many satisfactory hypotheses. The next question is how they can be tested. Modern research on adaptation uses three main methods, which we may begin by listing. The first is to show that the trait fits with what would have been expected to evolve, under natural selection, in its environment. The second method is experiment. The third is the comparison of many species to show that species consistently evolve the same kind of trait in a particular environment. As with all methods in science, the different methods are appropriate to different material.

Our original example of an adaptation—camouflage in moths—could illustrate both the first and second methods. The first is to show a fit between how the moths are and what could be predicted from the theory of natural selection. We can tell, by looking at a camouflaged moth, that its colour pattern is fitted to its environment. We could also predict that natural selection, if set to work on a population of moths, might produce moths that were difficult for predators to see. The argument in this case is easy, but the same general kind of research can produce less obvious results. Complicated engineering methods can be applied to the design of bones, or the shape of trees. We shall consider a subtle version of the engineer's method in an application to animal behaviour.

Different animals of the same population do not all behave identically. They show behavioural variation. One thoroughly studied case is that of the digging behaviour of the solitary wasp *Sphex ichneumoneus*. Females of this species lay their eggs in burrows in the ground. They provision the egg with food, in the form of some dead katydids (insects similar to crickets), which the larva eats after hatching. The behavioural variation in question, which is shown both by different females and by the same female on different occasions, concerns how the females obtain their burrows. They use two main methods. A female may either dig her own burrow or enter one dug by another female. That much is in her power; but her reproductive success is also influenced by whether she has her burrow to herself or shares it, which is determined by the behaviour of the other females in the population. A female may experience any of four fates when laying her eggs. She may dig and be alone or dig and be joined; and she may enter and be alone or enter and share (either because she joins, or is joined by, another female). For more than two females to share a burrow is sufficiently rare that it can be ignored.

Jane Brockmann has measured the successes of females of all four kinds. Because it takes time to dig a burrow, a female who enters a burrow that has been dug by another female is (conditionally—as we shall see) more successful than a female who digs her own. But females in shared burrows are less successful than lone females. The difference in success more than makes up for the cost of digging, for a female who digs a burrow and has it to herself leaves more offspring than one who enters a burrow but shares it. The ideal for a female is to enter a burrow and have the burrow to herself. But no female can guarantee the ideal for herself, because she may always have to share. Whether she has to share depends not on what she herself does, but what the other females in the population are doing.

The key to understanding how natural selection works on the system is that the advantages of the two female 'strategies', of 'digging' and 'entering', depend on what the other females in the population are doing. If most of the females are enterers, burrows will be in short supply and nearly all the enterers will have to share. The few digger-females will be at an advantage because they are less likely to have to share. But if most females are diggers, burrows will be abundant and enterers will have to share less. Enterers will now be at an advantage. Over evolutionary time, the proportions of the two different strategies will tend to adjust until they reach an equilibrium, with some of each. The equilibrium point is where neither strategy has an advantage over the other, because if one were doing relatively better, it would increase (over evolutionary time) until it stopped doing so.

In cases like this the appropriate method is game theory. John Maynard Smith is mainly responsible for introducing it into evolutionary biology; but in this case Brockmann collaborated with Alan Grafen and Richard Dawkins to apply game theory to the burrowing of *Sphex*. They calculated the proportion of diggers and enterers that would make the advantages of the two strategies equal; in one of the two populations studied the calculated proportion was just over 40 per cent enterers (and just under 60 per cent diggers): this should be the equilibrium point. They compared it with the actual proportions in nature. They studied two populations. In one the prediction was surprisingly good; in the other the model turned out to be inapplicable.

The method used with *Sphex* is fundamentally one of showing that the trait of the organism fits with what would be expected from natural selection. It is like looking at a camouflaged moth, and observing that the camouflage fits the environment; but the exact form of the method needed in the case of the wasps is much more sophisticated.

The second method of studying adaptation is experiment. In the normal method of science, the hypothesis must predict the result of altering the conditions. All hypotheses about adaptation, in principle, make scientific predictions; but in many cases they are practically impossible to test. Sometimes however this is not so. In both the examples that we have just discussed, the hypothesis could be tested by experiment. Taking the peppered moth *Biston betularia* first, if the camouflaged types were moved to a background against which they were conspicuous, the rate of predation should increase. Kettlewell performed exactly this experiment. He moved the peppered type from unpolluted to polluted areas, and the melanic type in the opposite direction; both types were then eaten more by birds. The results fitted the theory. He had experimentally confirmed the hypothesis of adaptation.

The digger wasp theory could also be tested experimentally. It predicts that if the proportion of one of the two strategies increases, it would become disadvantageous. The proportions of the strategies could in theory be altered, although it might be difficult in practice. Another experiment might be to fill in lots of burrows, which would change the relative advantages of the two strategies; their relative frequencies should adjust accordingly. Neither test has been done. They would probably be difficult to perform. For another case (there are only a few) of the experimental study of adaptation we must look elsewhere.

We may look to the evolution of clutch size in birds. Species of birds lay a characteristic average number of eggs per clutch. The average differs between species; in swifts, for example, in Great Britain it is two or three. But why is it two or three, and not one, five, six, or ten? David Lack suggested the following answer. Birds such as swifts not only have to lay their eggs, they also have to feed their young when they have hatched. The parental swifts bring back many small insects, such as green aphids, for their young; but the aphids take time to catch and bring to the nest. There will be a limit on how many the parents can bring. If the swifts laid too many eggs, they would not be able to provide for all the young; then, although they had laid more eggs, they would produce fewer live offspring. The hypothetical advantage is clearly to the individual pair of swifts, not to the group. There would be a group advantage in reducing reproduction in order not to over-eat the food supply. If swifts are restraining themselves only for the good of the group, then if they laid more eggs they should produce more live offspring.

Chris Perrins experimentally tested Lack's theory. He made use of the fact that one swift cannot tell its eggs from another's; if an extra egg is put in the nest it rears it like its own. He could therefore create artificially large clutches. Lack's theory predicts that the total number of surviving offspring from these nests should be lower than the total number from a normal nest, even though they have more eggs to start with. Perrins measured the survival rate of young from the normal and the experimental nests. He confirmed Lack's prediction: although the experimental nests started off with more eggs, they finished up with less offspring than a nest that started with three eggs. The reason was almost certainly that the parents could not provide for all the offspring. Lack's hypothesis of how clutch sizes are adaptive was experimentally confirmed.

The third method of studying adaptation is the comparison of many different species. It is a generalization of the first method. The first method was to show that the actual traits of species fit well with what we should predict from natural selection in the relevant circumstances. The comparative method examines whether different species, living in the same circumstances, predictably evolve the same trait. The body shape of sharks, for instance, may be an adaptation for swimming through water. Applying the first method, we should consider, in ever more detail, whether the body shape is indeed well designed for swimming. The second method might test the hydrodynamic properties of sharks, or model sharks, whose shape had been experimentally altered. The third method works as follows. The theory predicts the shape of animals that move by swimming through water. It can be tested by examining other species that move in this fashion, to see whether they too have the same body shape. If the theory is correct, they should. In this case, other such species—dolphins, whales, fish, even (perhaps) sea snakes—do indeed have much the same shape as sharks. The comparative evidence confirms the theory.

Comparison is most convincing when the species compared are of very different kinds. Then their similarity is likely to be convergent, rather than just being shared from a common ancestor. The similarity of dolphins to sharks is a more impressive confirmation of the theory than is the similarity of one species of shark to another. If the similarity is convergent, it has evolved independently in each case; each is an independent trial of the hypothesis of adaptation. The trials, being natural rather than experimental, are not (in a scientific sense) well controlled, but they can be used. The most powerful form of the comparative method is to count the number of times a trait has independently evolved in relation to the environment of its evolution. Only one such study has been done. It was done by me. Unfortunately it concerns a little-known habit; but it can illustrate the method.

The trait is a mating habit called a precopula. A precopula is a close physical association of the sexes, usually an actual embrace, before insemination; to count as a precopula it must last a reasonably long time (say, more than a day). Precopulas are found in many different invertebrate species, such as shrimps, crabs, spiders, mites, and one group of vertebrates, the Anura (frogs and toads). Other species do not have precopulas: the sexes, after meeting, either separate immediately (if they are not ready to mate) or mate straightaway. The question is why some species have precopulas but others do not. The hypothetical answer is that the species with precopulas share, in their reproductive cycles, another peculiar property which the species without precopulas lack: the females of species with precopulas can only be inseminated during a short (but predictable) interval of time. In the crabs with precopulas, for instance, each individual moults every few weeks, or months; but females can only be inseminated immediately after their moult. Just why this should be is uncertain, but it is a fact. In toads with precopulas, the breeding seasons tend to be concentrated in short 'explosive' intervals, when all the toads of a species may breed in a day or two.

The theory is this. If females can only be inseminated during a short interval, a male's chance of meeting her right in it will be low; in which case, if a male meets a female a short time before that interval, it may pay him to stay with her until she can be inseminated. By contrast, if a female can be inseminated at more or less any time, a precopulatory wait before mating can have no advantage. Again the hypothetical advantage is to the individual selfish male, who is selected to mate with as many females as possible.

And the prediction is this. Whenever a precopula has evolved, it should be in a species in which, for some reason, the females are only receptive for very short intervals of time. I tested it by the following method. I collected all the known facts about which species had, or did not have, a precopula, together with all the facts about the possible times of mating. From a knowledge of the evolutionary relations of the species, I then counted the minimum number of times that each of the four possible pairs of traits evolved. Here is the final result. Precopulas have evolved in species with a confined mating time on 19 occasions; they have evolved only once in a species with unconfined times of mating; the absence of precopula has evolved 10 times in species with an unconfined time of mating; and never at all in species with a confined time of mating. The facts, with only a single exception, fit the theory. The particular details of the numbers, and the mating habits concerned, are not important here. What matters is the method. By comparing cases of the independent evolution of a trait it is possible to test how it is an adaptation.

Such is the adaptationist's repertory of techniques. Each method can test how natural selection operates on a particular trait. But they all share a crucial assumption. They assume that the trait under study has been produced by natural selection. They assume that they are adaptations, and try to discover what kind of adaptation they are. The methods aim to identify the exact force of natural selection that was responsible for its evolution and maintenance.

The common assumption of the technical repertory may be an error. Is it correct to assume that all traits are adaptations? Could any traits evolve despite being useless to the organisms that carry them? Before we try to answer these questions, we should consider their meaning more carefully. The problem is to explain why organisms possess the particular traits they do rather than any others. We have seen how natural selection achieves this. We have seen why moths are camouflaged rather than conspicuous, why there is variation in the digging behaviour of wasps, why the clutch sizes of birds are what they are, and why mating in species in which the females have a limited period of reproductive receptivity is preceded by a precopulatory sexual association.

Adaptation implies that not all kinds of organism exist. If the molecules, or even the traits, of all the known species were mixed up at random, a huge variety of forms could be made. The few forms that naturally exist are only a small subset of the full range of possibilities. Some possibilities are not naturally realized. We may ask why not. One answer is that they are non-adaptive, that they are such things as dark moths on light backgrounds, which, when they exist, are selected against. They are absent because of negative selection.

For a trait to be favoured by natural selection, it must be a heritable variation. Then its frequency can increase over the generations. Similarly, if natural selection is to work against a trait, it must have existed as a heritable variation and been prevented from increasing in frequency in the population. If a non-adaptive form has never existed as a heritable variation, negative selection is not an appropriate explanation: it would be an explanation of something that never happened.

We have now reached a possible additional factor besides natural selection. Even before I state it, let me emphasize that it is not a true alternative to natural selection. As an explanation of adaptation, no alternative is known to natural selection. If one is to challenge the Darwinian theory of evolution by natural selection, there is little hope in challenging natural selection as an explanation of adaptation. One can only hope at best to be able to reduce its importance. If the traits of organisms are not all adaptations, natural selection could be confined to the undoubted adaptations. The theory that we are coming to does not seek to replace natural selection. That is impossible. It only seeks to cut it down to size.

Any particular non-existent form of life may owe its absence to one of two reasons. One is negative selection. The other is that the necessary mutations have never appeared. Some new mutations may never arise, because for some reason the range of genetically possible forms is constrained. We know that this is not true for melanic moths in unpolluted areas because melanic moths can be seen: the absence (which is only a relative absence in this case) is due to negative selection. But what of other absent forms, such as legged snakes or insects with backbones? Might their absence be due to constraint?

Four questions suggest themselves. The first is whether there is any constraint at all on genetic variation. There certainly must be, for as Maynard Smith has written, 'If there were no constraints on what is possible, the best phenotype [that is, kind of organism] would live for ever, would be impregnable to predators, would lay eggs at an infinite rate, and so on.' Such organisms do not exist. Their absence must be due to some kind of genetic constraint, because they would be favoured by natural selection if they ever arose: no question of negative selection here. Constraints do exist.

From here on we must become less conclusive, but we can at least pose three more questions. How widespread are constraints? Which particular traits (or their absence) are due to constraint? Why do constraints exist? Taking the first question first, we can only say that nature must lie between two extremes. Organisms are not perfectly adapted. This must be because the range of genetic variation is constrained. On the other hand, it is not extremely constrained. There is *some* heritable variation. Real organisms do not represent the only variants that have ever existed. Variation can be seen, for example, in artificial selection. If a population of cows are artificially selected to increase milk yield (for instance), milk yield increases over the generations. The increase is made possible by heritable variation for milk yield. In fact most traits must have heritable variants, because most properties of most species can be changed by artificial selection. The existence of adaptation (and no one doubts that *some* traits are adaptations) also proves the existence of genetic variation. Adaptations are produced by natural selection, and natural (like artificial) selection cannot work without genetic variation.

Organisms are not perfect, but nor are they completely non-adapted. They are somewhere between those two extremes. Unfortunately much room for disagreement extends between those extremes, most of which has been explored by biologists. We do not know how many non-existent forms are gaps in the genetical possibilities, and how many are excluded by negative selection. Some mutations are probably more likely than others, and some mutations so unlikely as to be impossible. We do not know enough to say which mutations are unlikely. We can only say that some are. In other words, we lack a precise theory of variation.

Although the problem is unsolved, we have a method to tackle it with. Indeed we have only just been discussing it. For any particular trait we can try to discover whether it is a possible genetic variant. The hypothesis of constraint states that any particular absent form, such as a legged snake, is genetically impossible. Now this is a testable hypothesis. We can try to produce a legged snake by artificial selection. If we succeed the hypothesis of constraint is wrong: if artificial selection can make a legged snake, so too could natural selection. If, however, we failed, then perhaps there is an inviolable constraint in the genetics or embryology of snakes that prevents the development of legs. The absence would then be due to the constraint, not to negative selection. Unfortunately this method can give only negative knowledge of constraints. It can tell us for a particular trait whether it is rigidly constrained. But if it turns out to be constrained we have not advanced in our understanding of why the constraint exists: we merely know that it does. If we are to understand why constraints exist, and why they have whatever form they do, we shall need a more positive programme of research. It will have to tackle the problem at the level of mechanism rather than (as in artificial selection) their consequences.

It will have to tackle the fourth question, of why constraints exist. At the moment, we must content ourselves with merely speculative reasons. Here, to finish with, are some speculations. It might be that certain mutations would interrupt some essential event early in the development of the organism. The series of events that cause an egg to develop into an adult are not known for any species; but it is possible that there are vital developmental events that cannot be changed. They would be developmental constraints, if they exist. According to what may be called structuralist embryology, such constraints are common, and are the reason why many kinds of organisms do not exist; but it is merely a hypothesis. Another kind of constraint might come from genetics: for some genetic reason, such as the chemical functions of the molecules of heredity, particular mutations may be prevented. This would be a genetic constraint. Whatever the content of a theory of variation turns out to be, the necessary knowledge will probably come from the study of developmental genetics. That (among other reasons) is why evolutionary biologists are interested in embryology. Interest, however, is not knowledge. The degree of constraint on the variation of organisms is not known. The problem remains.

5 Molecular Evolution

All the parts of organisms change during evolution. While the fins of fish evolved in amphibians into limbs, and they in turn evolved into many shapes and sizes, their constituent tissues, cells, and molecules were also changing. The evolutionary changes of molecules are the subject of this chapter. Molecular evolution will here usually be synonymous with protein evolution, because evolution at the molecular level has been most thoroughly studied in proteins.

Proteins are the commonest and most diverse class of molecules in organisms. A waterproof protein called keratin forms skin and hair; blood-clotting proteins called fibrinopeptins and an oxygen-carrying protein called haemoglobin circulate in the blood; many kinds of proteins, called enzymes, catalyse the metabolism of the body. There are many more; a human body contains thousands of kinds of proteins. All proteins are made of chains of amino acids. They are distinguished structurally, by the sequence of their chains. In natural proteins there are 20 different amino acids; different proteins differ only in the sequence of their amino acid chain. Haemoglobin, for instance, is a chain of 141 amino acids. The sequence is specific to haemoglobin, but differs slightly in different species: the sequences are similar enough to be recognizable as haemoglobin rather than any other kind of protein, but a few amino acids are not the same. The more distant the relative, the more amino acids differ. The haemoglobin of the Japanese monkey differs in four amino acids from human haemoglobin. The haemoglobin of a dog differs in 23. The sequence of haemoglobin has changed during evolution.

We shall be concerned with two kinds of facts about molecular evolution. Changes in amino acid sequences between species are one. The other is the variation of proteins within a species at any one time. Although it is true that human haemoglobin differs from that of the Japanese monkey by four amino acids, this only applies to the commonest type of haemoglobin in each. There is really no such thing as 'the' human haemoglobin. Over a hundred different forms of haemoglobin, differing ever so slightly in their amino acid sequences, are known in the human species. The co-existence of more than one variant of any trait, such as a protein, within a species is called polymorphism.

Polymorphism, however, has not been much studied at the level of amino acid sequence. It takes time to find out the sequence of one protein, but to sequence all the different forms of several proteins in several species would be practically impossible. Another method has been used. It is much quicker and rather cruder. It is called gel electrophoresis. Its principle and its method are as follows. Each amino acid has a characteristic electrical charge. A protein therefore has an electric charge equal to the total charge of all its constituent amino acids. Because proteins differ in their amino acids, they must differ in their electric charges. The charge determines how rapidly the protein will move in an electric field. A protein being subjected to gel electrophoresis is simply placed in an electric field, left for some time, and then stained to reveal how far it has moved. If there are different forms of the protein they will probably move different distances. They are distinguished by their electric charge, rather than directly by their amino acid sequence.

Electrophoresis cannot detect every different protein form. Not all amino acids differ in their electric charges. If two forms of a protein differ only in electrically identical amino acids, electrophoresis will not distinguish them. Indeed, it may only distinguish one third, or even less, of the variations of proteins. But although it is a crude method, when it was first used in 1966 to estimate the level of protein polymorphism, it led to an important and unexpected discovery. We shall discuss it soon. But before we come to the facts, we should establish their significance. Why worry about the polymorphisms and evolution of proteins? Why *molecules* rather than cells, or bones, or brains, or anything else?

The main reason is that molecular evolution has become the

sparring ground of one of the great controversies in evolution. In 1968 the Japanese genetical theoretician Motoo Kimura proposed his neutral theory of molecular evolution, and ever since then evolutionary biologists have been trying to find out whether the evolution of molecules is driven by natural selection or (as Kimura maintains) by random neutral drift. The alternatives can be called selectionism and neutralism: but what exactly do they mean? Selectionism should be clear enough, for in its general form it has been the subject of the last two chapters. Applied to molecules it means that molecular evolution is driven by natural selection. New forms of proteins (according to selectionism) are substituted in evolution only when they are favoured by natural selection. Neutralism offers a completely different explanation. It denies that most evolutionary changes are caused by selection. It suggests instead that most different forms of proteins are selectively equivalent: selection does not favour one over another. Evolution will then not be driven by selection, but by random drift. If there are two selectively equivalent forms of a protein in a population, one will eventually be established alone. Which one it is depends only on luck, not selection. Whereas according to selectionism different types of protein (or of anything) leave different numbers of offspring in different environments, according to neutralism the different types leave the same number of offspring.

Evolution by random drift is undoubtedly possible in theory. Thus, suppose that a selectively neutral mutation arose in a population. Initially it would be in a single copy. One might suppose that, because natural selection will neither eliminate it nor favour it, it would stay in a single copy. But in fact it is unlikely to stay as a single copy for long. As we have seen (p. 21), the genes of one generation are a random sample of those in the previous generation. Because more gametes are produced than can grow up, the surviving organisms must be only a sample of the gametes that could have survived. One form of a gene may be lucky in the sampling and drift upwards in frequency; after a few generations it may drift down again. If the alternative genes are selectively neutral with respect to each other, then on average neither will gain or lose through random drift.

For a single rare neutral mutation, the most likely effect of random drift is to eliminate it. If its frequency once drifts down to zero it is lost: it cannot drift up again if it does not exist. But the opposite result is possible. A series of lucky samples could carry its frequency up from one copy to become the only gene of its kind in the population. Obviously this is a very unlikely process, but if it is tried often enough it will eventually happen. Because we are simply dealing with the laws of probability, the chance that a neutral mutation will be established can be calculated. It turns out to be $1/2N$, N being the number of individuals in the population. No one doubts the calculation. It merely gives the chance that a neutral mutation will be established *if* one arises. In fact it may not: what is controversial is whether neutral mutations are common enough to account for the molecular evolution that has been observed.

Neutralism and selectionism are general ideas. They could apply equally to morphology and molecules. Many morphological differences have been suggested, at some time or other, to be selectively neutral. The fact that we are interested in the controversy of neutralism and selectionism, therefore, does not answer the question of why we are concerned with the evolution of molecules. Here is a better reason. Kimura only applies his theory to molecular evolution. He thinks that morphological evolution is driven by selection, but molecular evolution (for the most part) is not. Indeed, no important biologist believes that morphological evolution is mainly neutral.

There is a second reason for concentrating on molecules. The study of evolution has advanced much further for molecules than for morphology. More precise tests of ideas are possible. We might ask why. The answer, I think, is that we know the relation between any change in the amino acid sequence of a protein and the mutation that must have caused it. Mutations are changes in the structure of the hereditary material, DNA: when the DNA structure changes, it causes a change in the protein that is read off from it. Because the exact translation between DNA and protein is known, it is possible to estimate how many mutations were needed to produce any particular change in the proteins of two different species.

No comparable estimate can be made for such gross features of organisms as teeth and limbs. We can measure the differences between (for instance) the limbs of two species, but because the relation between limbs and the genes encoding them is not known, we cannot estimate how many mutations produced any particular change in a limb. We do not know whether the difference between a dog's leg and a bird's wing is produced by 300 or 30,000 genetic changes. But we know almost exactly how many mutations would change dog haemoglobin into chicken haemoglobin. The amount of genetic change is a crucial variable in the theory of evolution. Therefore, molecular evolution can be studied much more deeply than morphological.

Turning to the question of polymorphism, the study of molecules by gel electrophoresis has a different kind of advantage over the study of gross morphological features. The aim is to measure the average amount of genetic variation for all the genes of a species. There are too many genes—perhaps 10,000 in a human being—for it to be possible to measure the variation of all of them. We are forced to sample, and desire the sample to be as large and as representative as possible.

Gel electrophoresis has advantages both in scale and representation. It is quicker than the old-fashioned Mendelian study of gross traits. One could study many traits by the Mendelian method and obtain an estimate of how many genetic variants there are on average per trait per species. It would take a long time, that is all. The number of variants of a protein, however, can be measured quickly. Such is the advantage of scale. What is the advantage of representation? Let us compare a sample of (say) 30 proteins with one of 30 morphological traits. Which is more representative? Either sample would be biased if it tended to contain genes more or less variable than average. But there is a reason why the sample of proteins, analysed by gel electrophoresis, is less likely to be biased. Because we cannot see them in the animals before the analysis, unconscious selection is impossible. Morphological traits can be seen before being measured, which opens up the possibility of unconscious selection. Preconceptions, therefore, may have more influence on the measurement of morphology than of molecules. That is all we need say about the reason for studying molecules. Let us now turn to the facts and their differing neutralist and selectionist interpretations.

If the crucial difference between selectionism and neutralism is that according to the former the bearers of different protein types produce different numbers of offspring, in some specified environment, whereas according to the latter they produce equal numbers, the most direct test between them would be to measure the reproductive success of the bearers of different protein types. Unfortunately there is very little evidence of this kind. Industrial melanism in moths (p. 27) is an example. One type of the moth (melanic) is advantageous on one background and the other type (peppered) on another. Neutralism is wrong in this case. But the controversy will not be settled by this kind of evidence. There are too many proteins, and each one takes too long to study. The general theories of neutralism and selectionism refer to hundreds, even thousands, of proteins; evidence from a few (whichever theory it fits best) cannot decide between them. No neutralist would be worried by the demonstration of natural selection on one or two (or ten or twenty) proteins. Their theory does not deny that natural selection works on a few genes, especially those with gross and visible effects: it merely asserts that the great majority of molecular differences are selectively neutral. Nor do selectionists deny that a few genetic differences may be (at any rate temporarily) selectively neutral. They merely say that the majority are not. It is not a question of neutralism or selectionism, but of how much of each.

It is perfectly reasonable that the two theories should take that form. The extreme positions are almost certainly wrong, and no one can be blamed for not holding a theory which is almost certainly wrong. The trouble is that it makes them more difficult to test. We cannot test them with studies of single proteins. We have to work with more general, but less direct, evidence.

Kimura proposed his neutral theory because of three main kinds of evidence: the high rate of molecular evolution, the constancy of the rate, and the large amount of protein polymorphism. As to high rate, amino acid changes in proteins take place about once every thousand million years in haemoglobin, and 8.3 times per thousand million years in fibrinopeptins. Kimura argued that natural selection cannot drive evolution at so high a rate; but the argument is involved and inconclusive, and we shall not discuss it here. The constancy of molecular evolution provides a clearer argument. Amino acid changes appear to accumulate through evolutionary time at an approximately constant rate. If they are being incorporated into the molecule by natural selection, then it must be exerting an approximately constant force.

From the study of morphological evolution, evolutionary biologists had not supposed that the force of natural selection was constant through time. Morphological evolution takes place at an erratic rate. For the vertebrate limb, the transition from fin to tetrapod limb was completed in a few tens of millions of years in the Devonian and since then has changed little over long periods; when it evolved into the bird wing, the transition was again relatively abrupt and followed by a much longer period when the wing, after being completed, changed little. Changes took place quickly (but over many millions of years) and were followed by periods of stability. The pattern of molecular evolution is different. In a molecule like haemoglobin, changes occur at a fairly constant rate. (It is because of this difference between evolution in molecules and in gross morphology that Kimura applies his neutral theory only to molecules, and leaves the higher levels of the organism to natural selection.)

According to Kimura, molecular evolution has a constant rate because it is a process of neutral random drift. We have already noticed the chance that neutral mutation will be established in the population. It is $1/2N$. With that, it is easy to calculate the rate of neutral evolution. The rate of neutral evolution is simply the rate at which neutral mutations arise multiplied by the chance that one will become established. If neutral mutations arise at a rate m per gene, and there are two genes per individual, the total rate at which neutral mutations appear in the population is $2Nm$. The rate of neutral evolution is then $2Nm \times 1/2N$: the $2N$ cancel: the rate is simply m. The rate of neutral evolution is equal to the neutral mutation rate.

The rate of neutral evolution (equal to the neutral mutation rate) just given was the average rate. The important question is how variable the rate is. Mutation (as we have seen, p. 25) is random. Over a long period of time, the rate of a random process is approximately constant. Neutral evolution, therefore (if it occurs) should have an approximately constant rate. As we have seen, the rate of molecular evolution is approximately constant; but unfortunately this is not very strong evidence for the neutral theory. It is only a high-level fit between fact and theory. After all, natural selection might also drive molecular evolution at a constant rate. The force of natural selection on morphology and on molecules may differ. The constant rate of molecular evolution fits but does not prove the neutral theory.

Even with the high-level fit of fact and theory, there is a difficulty for the neutral theory. The rate of molecular evolution is approximately constant (even this has been challenged, but let that pass), but it is constant with respect to time, not the number of generations. Because the mutation rate is probably proportional to numbers of generations, and not of years, the neutral theory would predict faster molecular evolution in species with shorter generation times. But in fact, in all the molecules that have been studied, the rate of evolution does not depend on generation time: it is the same in mice and whales and rabbits and elephants. The neutral theory can only be saved by an *ad hoc* and implausible hypothesis, namely that (for some reason) neutral mutations, unlike other mutations, arise at a constant rate per year, not per generation.

We have so far considered the evolutionary changes of molecules through time. Let us now turn to protein polymorphism. The crucial observation, for the controversy of neutralism and selectionism, is the large amount of polymorphism that was revealed by gel electrophoresis. When the first studies were done in 1966, on the fruitfly *Drosophila* by Lewontin and Hubby and on humans by Harris, it was found that a large proportion of genes were polymorphic within a population. There are two main measures of variability, 'heterozygosity' and 'percentage polymorphism', of which the latter is easier to understand. It is simply the percentage of genes for which there is more form in the species. (If there is only one variant of a gene, it is called monomorphic.) Typical figures of percentage polymorphism for natural populations are about 25–50 per cent. The true figures must be even higher, for gel electrophoresis does not detect all variation.

How can this large amount of polymorphism be explained? Kimura has called the question 'the outstanding problem confronting present-day population genetics'. His neutral theory would offer the same kind of answer as for molecular evolution. The protein polymorphisms at any one time (it would say) are transient neutral forms, one of which is on its lucky way to establishment. A formula can be derived for the average amount of polymorphism that would be expected under neutral drift; but the derivation is too involved to work through here. The formula contains only the population size and the neutral mutation rate, neither of which are known for any species. By stuffing appropriate (but not altogether unrealistic) numbers in the formula, almost any level of polymorphism can be explained. The fit of fact and theory means that the neutral theory cannot be refuted by the simple observation of levels of polymorphism. But it is not a strong test because the theory is consistent with almost any level of polymorphism.

The theory of natural selection can also account for the facts. Three main ways are known by which natural selection can produce polymorphism. One is transient polymorphism. Transient polymorphisms exist while one genetic variant is increasing under natural selection in frequency and its alternative is decreasing. There will be a short interval of a few thousand generations after the appearance of a favoured mutant during which it replaces its alternative. If a population was sampled during that interval, polymorphism would be seen. Transient polymorphism is thought to explain only a tiny minority of polymorphisms because it is thought unlikely that improvements could be going on, at any one time, in many of the traits of a species.

A second circumstance on which natural selection favours polymorphism is when the heterozygote is favoured, a condition called heterozygous advantage. Consider the three genotypes of a gene that has two forms; conventionally they are called *AA*, *Aa*, *aa*. Heterozygous advantage means that *Aa* types leave more offspring than do *AA* and *aa*. When natural selection thus favours the heterozygote, the population will be polymorphic: it will contain both *A* and *a*. No one doubts that some polymorphism is maintained by heterozygous advantage. There is one well-known example of a haemoglobin variant that is maintained by it in some human populations; it is responsible for sickle cell anaemia. (In certain areas of West Africa, homozygotes for a normal haemoglobin gene are liable to catch malaria; homozygotes for the sickle cell haemoglobin gene die of anaemia; but heterozygotes are liable neither to malaria nor anaemia, and are therefore favoured.) What is controversial is whether heterozygous advantage could cause all, or even much of, the polymorphism of natural populations. One (of several) reasons for doubt is that in the bacterium *Escherichia coli* there is the usual high level of polymorphism even though the bacterium has only one copy of each of its genes (instead of the normal two, as in the ordinary Mendelian inheritance of the pea). The polymorphism of *E. coli* cannot be due to heterozygous advantage because it does not have heterozygotes. We need another explanation in *E. coli*, and what serves for *E. coli* may well serve for other species as well. Of course, it may not: *E. coli* may be a special case. We are assuming that a general explanation can be found, rather than a variety of different explanations for different species.

The third mechanism is frequency-dependent selection. We have met it before when discussing the adaptations of digger wasps. Frequency-dependent selection means that the advantage of a type depends on its frequency in the population. Negative frequency-dependence is necessary to maintain polymorphism; that is, as the frequency of the type increases, its advantage must decrease. Then, if one type increases in frequency, natural selection will work against it and in favour of its alternative. The proportions will return to their polymorphic equilibrium.

Natural selection, by some combination of these three mechanisms, can account for the polymorphism of proteins. The mere observation of polymorphism, therefore, cannot by itself decide between the theories. That completes our examination of Kimura's original three arguments for his neutral theory. None of them are conclusive. Some other test is needed.

A recent discovery suggests that at least a certain class of molecular evolution is neutral. Apart from the fact that the evidence is relatively conclusive (although this might be challenged), it is also worth discussing because it illustrates an important refinement of the neutral theory. The version of neutralism that we have been discussing so far is a crude simplification, which Kimura calls the theory of pan-neutrality. Pan-neutrality states that all the different forms of a protein are neutral alternatives. There is evidence that pan-neutrality is wrong; and, as we see how Kimura deals with the evidence, we shall also discover his more refined neutral theory.

The evidence concerns synonymous mutations. The code of inheritance is written in triplets of molecules called bases. There are four different bases (symbolized A, C, G and U) and 64 different triplets. Each triplet encodes a single amino acid. Because there are only 20 amino acids, the code is triply redundant. Some base changes do not produce amino acid changes; these are the synonymous mutations. An example of a synonymous mutation is the change from the base sequence GCU to GCC, both of which code for the same amino acid, alanine: a mutation from GCU to GCC will not cause a change in the amino acid sequence of the protein. Neutralists had been saying for many years that synonymous mutations are selectively neutral; but a test did not become possible until DNA sequencing methods were developed in the 1970s. The tests with DNA sequences are powerful. The very first one that we can perform is enough to destroy pan-neutralism. It goes like this. If synonymous changes really are neutral, then the different synonymous bases should be present in approximately equal proportions. GCU, GCC, GCA, and GCG, for example, all encode alanine; if it does not matter which is used they should be equally abundant. Now, are they? We have evidence for three species: *E. coli*, yeast, and man. In *E. coli* the four are in approximately equal proportions; but in yeast and man there are gross disproportions, GCU and GCC being much commoner than GCA and GCG. When all the synonymous changes are considered together, the frequencies of different triplets are extremely non-random. The only escape for the theory of pan-neutrality would be to hope that the different triplets have different mutation rates. But that is a forced explanation, supported neither by evidence nor probability. We may conclude that pan-neutralism is false. The synonymous triplets are not selectively equivalent.

Natural selection can account for the facts. The selectionist would say that for some reason the more frequently found triplets are more often favoured by selection; mutations of the favoured class are therefore driven into the population by natural selection. It would have to be left for later research to find out exactly why some triplets are more often favoured, but in the meantime plenty of hypotheses could be offered.

Now we can come to Kimura's neutral theory. This explains different rates of molecular evolution by differences in the degree of selective constraint. It had long been known, for instance, that rates of evolution in enzymatic proteins are slower in the 'active site', the part of the protein where its function is carried out, than in the outlying parts. Kimura explains this by supposing that the exact amino acids are crucial in the active site, but not so crucial elsewhere in the molecule. Changes are more likely to be neutral away from the active site, where evolution accordingly is faster. Evolutionary changes, when they occur, are still neutral, but neutral changes are not equally likely in all parts of the molecule.

This may look like saving the neutral theory by turning it into selectionism, but it is not. To understand why, we need the distinction between the negative and positive forms of natural selection. Negative selection (p. 55) acts to prevent disadvantageous mutations from increasing in frequency; the increase in frequency of an advantageous mutation is due to positive selection. Armed with that distinction we can re-state the distinction between Kimura's neutral theory and selectionism. Both theories agree on the existence of negative selection: both agree that some mutations are disadvantageous, and that the reason why they are not found in natural populations is that negative selection keeps them out. The difference between the theories concerns only the cause of evolutionary changes. Selectionism asserts that evolution is driven by positive natural selection; Kimura's neutral theory that it is driven by random drift.

Let us return to those synonymous triplets. GCU and GCC have higher frequencies than GCA and GCG. Pan-neutrality cannot explain these unequal frequencies. Natural selection can. But what of Kimura's neutral theory? It too can explain them. It would say that GCA and GCG have low frequencies because there is often negative selection against them. Mutations from GCC or GCU to GCG or GCA are not neutral: they are disadvantageous. Mutations from GCC to GCU (and back) are according to Kimura's theory neutral: whenever one was substituted for the other during evolution, it was by random drift. The relative frequencies of synonymous triplets can no longer test between neutralism and selectionism. We are led back to the crossroads again. Now that we have incorporated the idea of negative selection into neutralism, it has become as vague and versatile as selectionism. It can explain any relative frequencies of genes, or base triplets, by declaring that negative selection is at work.

The evidence from relative frequencies of synonymous triplets refuted the theory of pan-neutrality, but has left us with selectionism and Kimura's neutral theory. To test between them we must turn to another property of the base triplets: the rates of evolution at its different positions. A triplet has a first position, a second position, and a third position. The genetic code is such that nearly all the synonymous changes are concentrated in the third position. In other words, a change in the first or second position nearly always changes the amino acid encoded; but in the third position it often does not. The third position (according to Kimura) is therefore less selectively constrained; negative selection is relaxed. If he is right, it should evolve at a higher rate than the other two. Kimura actually made this prediction in 1968, but it was not possible to test it even provisionally until a decade later. The facts so far have turned out in his favour. The rate of evolution is much higher in the third position than in the other two, which can be most easily explained if synonymous changes are selectively neutral. Selectionists had imagined reasons why synonymous changes might not be neutral, but none of them had ever predicted that evolution would actually be faster than average for synonymous changes.

Pseudogenes provide similar evidence. A pseudogene is (probably) a molecular equivalent of the appendix in humans. It is a functionless vestige of a formerly functional gene; for instance, some pseudogenes lack one of the parts that are needed for a gene to be translated into a protein. If the gene is not translated, it must lie dormant inside its bearer. Then, according to the neutral theory, all negative selection would be removed and the genes should be free to evolve at a very high rate. But what are the facts? The little that is known indicates that pseudogenes have high rates of evolution. That fits neutralism, but is there a selectionist explanation? It is difficult to imagine one. Why should positive natural selection drive particularly fast evolution in a molecule that has no function? It is only easy to imagine, with the neutralist, why selection should not prevent fast evolution. In fact the rate of evolution in pseudogenes is even higher than among synonymous third bases, which suggests that those synonymous changes are to some extent constrained by negative selection.

The high rate of evolution in pseudogenes and synonymous base changes is best explained as, for the most part at least, neutral drift. But we are still left with the problem of explaining molecular evolution as a whole. If these two cases were representative of all molecular evolution, we could conclude that the neutral theory is correct. But we cannot say that they are representative. They may be exceptional. Like the minority of cases in which natural selection has been confirmed, they do not solve the problem as a whole. The two theories are rather versatile at the level at which observations can be made, which makes it difficult to test them. We should conclude that, although the study of molecular evolution is more precise than many other aspects of evolution, it is not yet precise enough. The controversy of neutralism and selectionism has not been resolved.

6 Principles of Classification

What is the proper relation of the theory of evolution and the classification of living things? The strongest possible relation would be one of practical necessity, if classification were practically impossible without the theory of evolution. The facts of history alone show that this relation does not hold. People had successfully classified animals and plants for two millennia before evolution was ever accepted. The simplest act of classification, indeed, requires no theory at all, let alone the theory of evolution; it merely requires that groups be recognized, defined, and named. A group, in this simple sense, is a collection of organisms that share a particular defining trait; the group Chordata for instance contains all animals that possess a notochord, a hollow dorsal nerve chord, and segmented muscles. Classification, as the definition and naming of groups, is in principle easy, but it is also important. It is even essential. Biologists could not communicate or check their discoveries if their specimens had not been classified into publicly recognized groups.

If communication were the only purpose of classification it would not matter what groups were defined, provided that the definitions were agreed upon. Chordata happens to be a group that is generally recognized, but by the same method we could define other groups that are not normally recognized. We might, for instance, define the Ocellata as the group of all living things that possess eyes. It would contain most vertebrates, many insects and crustaceans, some molluscs and worms, and some other odd invertebrates. The Ocellata has not, so far as I know, ever been considered as a taxonomic group; but, if classification is only a matter of defining and naming groups, we might ask why it is not.

That question brings us to the fundamental problem of classification. Different traits define different groups. We could just accept some groups and not others. We could agree that Ocellata is intrinsically as good a group as Chordata, but declare that it just so happens that we have decided to recognize Chordata but not Ocellata. Classification would then be subjective. And if that satisfied us, evolution would not only be practically unnecessary but completely unnecessary, for there would be no more to classification than its practice.

Most biologists, however, are not so easily satisfied. They would prefer the choice of groups to be principled rather than subjective. Then, if we do recognize Chordata but not Ocellata, it must be because some principle shows that the Chordata are an acceptable group, but the Ocellata are not. A perfect principle would unambiguously show whether any group was acceptable, and admit no conflict between acceptable groups. No groups would then be chosen subjectively: they would all be chosen by reference to the principle. Even in the absence of a perfect principle, a principle might still be useful if it narrowed down the number of groups that were acceptable. Once the need for a principle of the choice of traits is recognized, a third relation of the theory of evolution and classification is opened up between practical necessity and complete dispensability. If evolution supplied the only valid principle of choosing traits it would be philosophically necessary for classification, or if merely one among several principles, philosphically desirable. We have seen that evolution is practically unnecessary: from now on we shall be concerned with whether it is philosophically necessary, philosophically desirable, or completely unnecessary.

We can assume that the classification of life will at all events be hierarchical. A hierarchical classification (as we saw in Chapter 1) is one whose groups are contained completely within more inclusive groups, with no overlap: humans (for example) are contained within the genus *Homo*, which is contained within the order of primates, which is contained within the class Mammalia, which is contained within the sub-phylum Vertebrata, which is within the phylum Chordata, which is within the kingdom Animalia. In principle biological classifications might not be hierarchical, but in practice they nearly all are. We are not ignoring a contentious practical issue.

What, then, could supply a principle for the hierarchical classification of life? Two kinds of answer have been offered: a *phenetic* hierarchy, or a *phylogenetic* one. A phenetic hierarchy is one of the similarity of form of the groups being classified; it is defined by any traits, such as leg length, skin colour, number of spines on back, or some collection of them. A phylogenetic hierarchy is one of the pattern of evolutionary descent; groups are formed according to recency of common ancestry.

The phenetic and phylogenetic principles may agree or disagree, according to the species considered. Figure 4 shows the phenetic and phylogenetic relations of three sets of three species. The phenetic and phylogenetic classifications are the same if the rate of evolution is approximately constant and its direction is divergent, as is probably true of a human, a chimp, and a rabbit (Figure 4a): the human and the chimp share a more recent common ancestor and resemble each other more closely than does either with the rabbit. The two principles disagree when there is convergence or differential rates of divergent evolution. A barnacle, a limpet, and a lobster illustrate the case of convergence (Figure 4b): the barnacle and limpet are phenetically closer, but the barnacle has a more recent common ancestor with the lobster. The barnacle has converged, during evolution, on to the molluscan form. The salmon, lungfish, and cow illustrate the other source of disagreement (Figure 4c): a lungfish is phenetically more like a salmon than a cow; but it shares a more recent common ancestor with a cow than with a salmon. The evolutionary line leading from lungfish to cows has changed so rapidly that cows now look utterly different from their piscine ancestors. Lungfish indeed have hardly changed at all in 400 million years; they are often called living fossils.

Clearly, evolution is a necessary assumption of phylogenetic classification: if organisms did not have evolutionary relations, we could not classify according to them. But evolution is not an assumption of the phenetic system: we could classify organisms by their similarity of appearance whether they shared a common ancestor or had been separately created. In the phenetic system, classification is by similarity of appearance, not evolution. If the phylogenetic principle is invalid, evolution will be completely

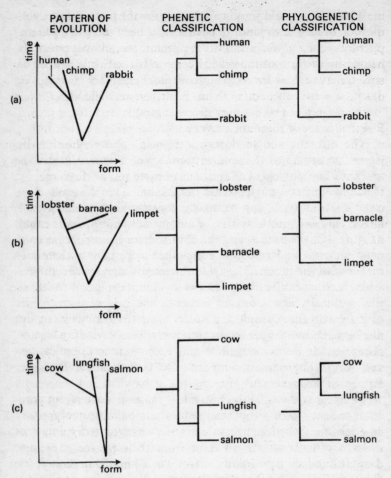

Fig. 4. Phenetic and phylogenetic classification.

The pattern of evolution (left), phenetic classification (centre), and phylogenetic classification (right) for three cases. Phenetic and phlyogenetic classification agree in the case of (a) human, chimp, and rabbit; but disagree when there is convergence, as in the case of (b) barnacle, limpet, and lobster, or when there is differential divergence, as in the case of (c) salmon, lungfish, and cow.

unnecessary in classification; if both principles are valid, evolution will be philosophically desirable; if only the phylogenetic principle is valid, evolution will be philosophically necessary. If neither principle is valid, we shall have to fall back on the kind of subjectivity that we aimed to escape from. Such is the significance of the question of whether the two principles are valid.

Phenetic and phylogenetic classification have each grown into a whole school, complete with its own philosophical self-justifications, techniques, and advocates. Phenetic classification is advocated by the school of numerical taxonomy; phylogenetic by the school called cladism. There is another important school of classification as well. It is a school often called evolutionary taxonomy, whose practitioners are more numerous than either numerical or cladistic taxonomy. But despite its importance, we need not concern ourselves with it here. Its hierarchical classifications mix phenetic and phylogenetic components; the 'evolutionary' classification of the barnacle, limpet, and lobster is phylogenetic, but of lungfish, salmon, and cow is phenetic. In covering the pure extremes, we shall cover the arguments of the mixed school too. What we want to know are the justifications of numerical taxonomy, which should justify phenetic classification, and of cladism, which should justify phylogenetic classification. Let us take phenetic classification first.

We have already met the difficulty of classification by an arbitrarily chosen trait. It is that some traits define some groups, other traits other groups; eyes defined the (customarily unrecognized) Ocellata, notochords the (customarily recognized) Chordata. If our only principle is to pick traits and define groups by them, we are left with a subjective choice among conflicting groups like Ocellata and Chordata. The numerical taxonomic school, which flourished from the late fifties into the sixties, believed that it had an answer to this problem. It would classify not by single traits, but by as many traits as possible. It would study dozens, even hundreds, of traits, which it would then average in order to define its groups. It came with a repertory of statistical procedures designed to realize that end. The general kind of statistic is what is called a multivariate cluster statistic. Given many measurements of many traits in the units to be classified, the cluster statistic averages all the measurements, to form groups (or 'clusters') of units according to their similarity in all the traits. The groups in the classification are said to be defined by their 'overall morphological similarity'. It was believed that if many traits were used, the groups discerned by the cluster statistic would be less arbitrary. Whereas groups defined by a few different traits may contain very different members, as did Chordata and Ocellata, groups defined by a large number of traits (it was thought) would have more consistent memberships.

We must consider a cluster statistic in more detail. The clusters are formed according to what is called the 'distance' between the units being classified. A distance in this sense is not the distance from one place to another, such as five miles, but is the difference between the values of a trait in two groups. Suppose that we are classifying two species. If the legs of one species are on average six inches long and those of the other four inches, the distance between the two species with respect to leg length is two inches. Numerical taxonomy, however, does not operate with only one trait. It uses dozens. The distance between the groups is therefore measured as the average for all the traits. If we had also measured skin colour in the two species and the distance between the colours had been 0.3 units, then the average distance for the leg length and skin colour combined is $(2 + 0.3)/2 = 1.15$ units. This figure is called the 'mean trait distance'; it would also be possible to use the Euclidean distance, which is measured, in two dimensions, by Pythagoras's theorem. The method can be applied for an indefinitely large number of traits and species (or whatever unit). The cluster statistic can then set to work.

The cluster statistic forms groups (or 'clusters') by successively aggregating the units with the shortest distances to each other. It forms a hierarchy of clusters as more and more distant units are added in. The numerical taxonomy, or phenetic classification, of the species will then be exactly defined. The classification *is* the hierarchic output of the statistic.

The advantages which numerical taxonomy claims for itself are its objectivity and repeatability. Any taxonomist could take the same group of animals or plants, measure many traits quantitatively, feed the measurements into the cluster statistic, and the same classification would always emerge. Numerical taxonomists claimed that by contrast the methods used to reconstruct phylogenetic trees were hopelessly vague and woolly. We have not yet come to those techniques; but we can look now at how well the method of numerical taxonomy stands up by its own criterion. Is numerical taxonomy, and its resulting phenetic classification, really objective and repeatable?

The answer is that it is not. The reason is abstract, but too important to ignore. It was pointed out most powerfully by an Australian entomologist, L. A. S. Johnson, in 1968. When I wrote above that the cluster statistic simply forms a hierarchy by adding in turn the next least distant group, I ignored a problem. There is more than one cluster statistic, because there is more than one way of recognizing the 'nearest' group. As we shall see, these different cluster statistics define different groups. If numerical taxonomy is truly objective, its own principle must dictate which cluster statistic should be used and which classificatory groups recognized. If it does not its own claim to repeatability will be exploded. It will be hoist on its own petard.

We can illustrate the point by two different statistics, called a nearest neighbour statistic and an average neighbour statistic. These are just two among many, which makes the real problem even worse than what follows; but we can use only two statistics to illustrate the nature, if not the extent, of the problem. Nearest neighbour statistics form successively more inclusive groups by combining the sub-groups with the nearest neighbour to each other. We can see it in Figure 5, along with the average neighbour statistic, which forms more inclusive groups not from those sub-groups with the nearest *nearest* neighbour, but from those with the nearest *average* neighbour.

In Figure 5, the nearest neighbour and average neighbour cluster statistics produce different hierarchies. In many cases the two statistics will produce hierarchies of the same shape, even if they do differ quantitatively. But sometimes they will not. The two statistics then give different classifications. (The Figure only has two dimensions, which might be, say, leg length and skin colour; as we have seen, numerical taxonomists rely on many more than

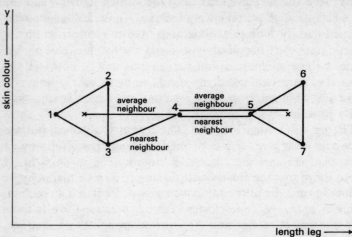

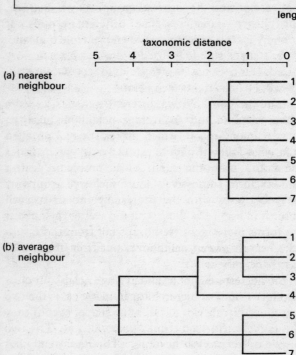

two traits. But that simplification is only to fit the printed page; it does not matter for the general point. Indeed the problem grows worse as more dimensions are introduced).

The principle of numerical taxonomy provides no guidance among the different cluster statistics. It implies no criterion by which to choose among the different hierarchies produced by different statistics. The principle of numerical taxonomy is to classify according to 'overall morphological similarity', but overall morphological similarity can only be measured by a cluster statistic. There is no higher measure of overall morphological similarity against which the different cluster statistics can be compared. When different statistics conflict, the practical numerical taxonomist has to decide which one he prefers. He can make a choice, of course; but it will have to be subjective.

The principle of phenetic classification, therefore, is a failure. Numerical taxonomy successfully removed subjectivity from the choice of traits, but only to see it pop up again (in a less obvious but equally destructive form) in the choice of cluster statistic. If phenetic relations cannot provide a valid principle for the hierarchical classification of living things, what about phylogeny?

Here there is more hope. Unlike the hierarchy of phenetic resemblance (or overall morphological similarity), the phylogenetic hierarchy does exist independently of our techniques to measure it. The phylogenetic tree is a unique hierarchy. It really

---

Fig. 5. Two cluster statistics in disagreement.

Seven species (nos. 1–7) have been measured for two traits, leg length and skin colour, and plotted in a two-dimensional space, with their leg length on the x-axis and their skin colour on the y-axis. Two cluster statistics, a nearest neighbour statistic and an average neighbour statistic, have been used to classify the seven species. The resulting classifications are shown below: (a) by nearest neighbour (b) by average neighbour. Both statistics first recognize the two groups, one of species 1, 2, 3, and the other of species 5, 6, 7. They disagree about the classification of species 4. The nearest neighbour statistic joins it to the group with the nearest *nearest* neighbour: it compares the two distances labelled nearest neighbour: the one to species 5 is shorter: species 4 is classified with species 5, 6, and 7 (classification (a)). The average neighbour statistic joins it to the group with the nearest *average* neighbour. The two points marked x are the average distances from species 4 to each group. The average neighbour statistic compares the two distances labelled average neighbour: the distance to the group of species 1, 2, and 3 is shorter, and species 4 is therefore classified with them (classification (b)).

is true, of any two species, that they either do or do not share a more recent common ancestor with each other than with another species. In phylogenetic classification, there is no problem of subjective choice among different possible hierarchies. There is only one correct phylogeny. If the evidence suggests that one classification is more like it than another, that is the classification to choose. The Chordata are allowed, but the Ocellata are not, because the group of chordates share a common ancestor but the group of species that possess eyes do not. Sometimes there will not be enough evidence to say whether one classification is more phylogenetic than another: then we should either have to make a provisional subjective choice, or refuse to choose until more evidence becomes available. The advantage of the phylogenetic principle is that it does possess a higher criterion to compare the evidence with: the phylogenetic hierarchy. This advantage had been vaguely understood by many evolutionary taxonomists, but it was first thoroughly thought through by the German entomologist Hennig. Cladism is sometimes called Hennigian classification.

Now that we have solved the philosophical problem we are left with the practical one. How can phylogenetic relations be discovered? Evolution took place in the past. Unlike phenetic relations, phylogenetic relations cannot be directly observed. They have to be inferred. But how?

For each species, we need to know which other species it shares its most recent common ancestor with, for that is the species with which it should be classified. How can we discover it? The method proposed by Hennig (and previously applied by many others) is to look for traits that are evolutionary innovations. During evolution, traits change from time to time. According to whether a particular trait is an earlier or a later evolutionary stage, it can be called a primitive or a derived trait. Most traits pass through several stages in evolution, and whether a particular stage is primitive or derived depends on which other stage it is being compared with: it is primitive with respect to later stages, but derived with respect to earlier ones. Consider as an example the evolution of the vertebrate limb. The most primitive stage is its absence; then, in fish, it appears as a fin; in amphibians the fin evolves into the tetrapodan pentadactyl (five-digit) limb; it has stayed like that in most vertebrates, but in some lizards and independently in some ungulates the number of digits on the limb has been reduced from five to four, three, two, or even (in horses) one. If we compare amphibians with fish, the pentadactyl limb is the derived state and fins the primitive state of this trait; but if we compare an amphibian with a horse, the five-toed state becomes primitive and the one-toed state in the horse is now the derived. Similarly if we compare the hand of a human with the front foot of a horse, the pentadactyl human hand is in the primitive state relative to the single-toed equine foot.

Such is the meaning of primitive and derived states. The distinction is necessary, in Hennig's system, in order that the derived traits can be selected for use in classification. The derived traits are selected because shared derived traits indicate common ancestry, whereas shared primitive traits do not. Let us stay with the same example. Suppose that we wish to classify a five-toed lizard, a horse, and an ape in relation to each other. The ape and the lizard share the trait 'five-toed', but this does not indicate that they share a more recent common ancestor than either does with the horse: the trait is primitive and does not indicate common ancestry within the group of horse, ape, lizard. Whenever there is an evolutionary innovation, it is retained (until the next evolutionary change) by the species descended from the innovatory species: shared derived traits do indicate common ancestry. That is why they are used to discover phylogenetic relations.

We can now move a further step in the search for a method. The problem has now become to distinguish primitive from derived traits. In the case of the vertebrate limb we assumed that the course of evolution was known. But how could it be discovered to begin with? There are several techniques. We need not consider them all. Let us look at one in detail to demonstrate that the distinction can be made. Let us consider outgroup comparison. The simplest case has one trait, with two states, in two species; lactation and its absence, for instance, in a horse and a toad. The problem is whether lactation in horses is derived with respect to its absence in toads, or its absence in toads is derived with respect to its presence in horses. The solution, by outgroup comparison, is obtained by examining the state of some related species, called the outgroup. The outgroup should be a species which is not more closely related to one of the two species than the other, that is why it is an *out*group: it is separated from the species under consideration. In this case any fish or invertebrate would do but a cow would not, because it is more closely related to the horse than it is to the toad. By the method of outgroup comparison, that trait is taken to be primitive which is found in the outgroup. Whether we took a species of fish or an invertebrate, the answer would be the same. The outgroup lacks lactation: lactation is the derived state.

The result of outgroup comparison is uncertain. It will be wrong whenever there is unrecognized convergence. Thus if we compared the trait 'body shape' in dolphins and dogs with some such outgroup as a fish we should determine that the dog had the derived shape. Actually the dolphin does. No one would be mistaken in the case of dolphins and fish; but other more subtle cases of convergence surely exist which are not as easy to recognize, and in them outgroup comparison will be misleading. But although it can go wrong, it is probably better than nothing. Shared traits are probably more often due to common ancestry than to convergence: but only more often, not always.

Advocates of phenetic classification often remark that phylogenetic classification is impossible because its techniques are circular. In the case of outgroup comparison, for instance, in order to apply the technique we needed to know that the outgroup (the fish) was less related to the toad and the horse than either to each other. It appears that we need to know the classification before we can apply the techniques; which would be quite a problem since the technique is supposed to be used to discover the classification. The problem, however, is not as destructive as it appears.

The argument of outgroup comparison is not circular. It works by what is often called successive approximation. It is the method by which theories are developed in all sciences. As new facts are collected and considered, they are examined in the light of the present theory. If they fit it, confidence in the theory is increased. If they do not, they may suggest a new theory, which can be used in considering yet further evidence. There is a continual reexamination of the theory in the light of new evidence, and when the theory is changed, our interpretation of all previous evidence should change too. This is not circular reasoning: it is testing a theory. In outgroup comparison, we can start with some crude idea of which species is an outgroup; if further evidence fits the crude idea, the hypothesis is (tentatively) confirmed, and it can then be used in interpreting further facts. Let us consider a hypothetical example.

Let us suppose that we have six species, and we suspect that one of them is less closely related than the other five. That one can be used as an outgroup. Comparison with it can be used to classify the other five, whose relations are not yet known. We first examine a trait in all six species. We take the state in the outgroup to be primitive for the group of five. Figure 6 shows the procedure. There are two points to notice. One is that the procedure can start from a very vague starting point; we do not need a firm classification to apply outgroup comparison. The other is that, if further evidence demands it, we can modify our initial ideas. If one trait after another suggests that species 6 is *not* separate from 1–5 then we can modify the classification, and put 6 in its appropriate place. All the previous steps would then have to be reconsidered. As the analysis proceeds any error at the beginning has a decreasing effect; the initial errors are gradually discovered, and their damaging consequences removed. Such is the method of successive approximation. It is the common method of scientific theory-building: only sciences that completely lack theories can do without the feedback between the interpretation of facts and the testing of theories.

Outgroup comparison is not the only cladistic method. Another method supposes that, as the organism develops, the evolutionarily derived stages appear after the primitive stages. The backbone of vertebrates is a derived state relative to its absence in invertebrates; and the backbone develops after its absence in a vertebrate embryo. Like outgroup comparison, the embryological criterion is imperfect but better than nothing. Another method is to look at the order in which the traits appear in the fossil record. The most powerful technique is to take all these methods together, and use all the evidence available. I do not wish to give the impression that the techniques of reconstructing phylogeny

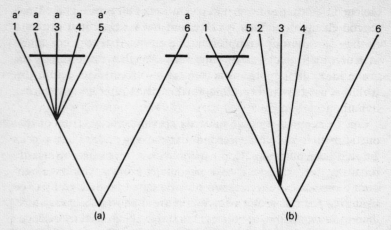

Fig. 6. Outgroup comparison by successive approximation.

(a) Five species (nos. 1–5) are to be classified, and it is thought that another species (6) is less related to them than any of the five to each other. Trait *A* is compared in all six species: species 2, 3, and 4 have it in state *a*, as does species 6, but species 1 and 5 have another state *a'*; by outgroup comparison *a'* is reasoned to be a derived state. (b) Species 1 and 5 are classified together, for they share a derived trait. The relations of species 2, 3, and 4 remain unknown; but the procedure can be repeated when evidence for new traits becomes available.

are perfect. They are far from that. Many problems remain, especially that of how to reconcile conflicting information from different traits. But although the system has difficulties, it is probably not altogether impractical. The cladistic evidence suggests that humans share a more recent common ancestor with chimps than with butterflies, and few biologists would deny that the evidence is correct in this case.

Derived traits, therefore, can be distinguished from primitive ones. Groups can be defined by shared derived traits. The cladistic system of phylogenetic classification is workable. But although cladistic groups can be recognized and defined, and although the classification (so far as it is phylogenetic) will be philosophically sound, it will only be valid for any one time. Evolution is continually going on; the traits of lineages continually change. What will define a group at one time may not define it at another. The traits defining groups are temporararily contingent, not essential.

Biological groups do not have Aristotelian 'essences'. The phylogenetic group Vertebrata may happen to be defined, at present, by the possession of bones (or cartilage), but that may no longer be true in a million years' time. A descendant of a vertebrate species may lack bones, and the trait will cease to define the evolutionary group. The traits that define groups are not eternal and inevitable: they just happen to be useful sometimes.

For the same reason, difficulties arise when species from different times (particularly fossils and present-day species) are put in the same classification. It can be done, but it is often awkward. Because traits are continually changing, groups with members from more than one geological period cannot be defined by constant traits. Furthermore, because (as we shall see in the next chapter) species may vary in space, the traits used in a classification strictly only apply to one place. But spatial variation, being more limited than temporal variation, is less of a practical problem. Spatial and temporal changes in traits are both only difficulties in the practice, not in the philosophy, of phylogenetic classification. The phylogenetic relations of a species remain real. The difficulty is in their discovery; phylogenetic relations have to be inferred from shared derived traits. But because traits do not remain constant in time and space, they are not perfectly reliable guides to the true phylogenetic relations of a species.

Because phylogenetic classifications are defined by shared traits, it is tempting to think that phylogenetic classification is really a form of phenetic classification. There is a measure of truth in this idea. Phylogenetic classification is defined by shared traits, and to that extent is phenetic. But it could not be otherwise. All classifications are phenetic in this sense. The proper description of a classificatory system as phylogenetic or phenetic should not be according to the techniques that it uses, but the hierarchy that it seeks to represent. There is an utterly different philosophy behind the two systems. One tries to represent the branching pattern of evolution; the other tries to represent the pattern of morphological similarity.

Moreover, different *kinds* of traits define phylogenetic and phenetic classifications. Phylogenetic classification supposes that some traits—shared derived traits in particular—are better indicators of phylogeny than are others. Phylogenetic classification, at least of the cladistic variety, uses only shared derived traits. Phenetic classification, by contrast, indiscriminately uses both primitive and derived traits. Both for reasons of philosophy and technique therefore it is misleading to call phylogenetic classification a form of phenetic classification.

Phylogenetic classification is philosophically preferable to its only competitor, phenetic classification. It is also a practical possibility. Its main problems are in its techniques, which are (as yet) far from perfect. But the techniques of cladism have been improved, even within their short history, and further work, particularly on molecules, should improve them further. The difficulty in phenetic classification is more fundamental. Its claim to preference, which is its objectivity, is a false claim. It is left with little to recommend itself by. Phenetic classification should, I think, be avoided whenever possible. Classifications, if they are to be objective, must represent phylogeny.

If this conclusion is correct, evolution and classification are closely related. The relation is one of philosophical necessity. Evolution is required to justify the kind of classification that is practised. Evolution is not merely desirable, but necessary, because phylogeny is the only known principle of classification. If we were content with merely subjective classification, evolution would be unnecessary. But if we are not—if we seek a principled classification—evolution becomes essential. It underwrites the entire philosophy of phylogenetic classification. Without evolution, phylogenetic classification, and its method of searching for derived traits, would be as subjective as any other technique. Only because we can assume that evolution is true (after Chapter 1), can we even begin to think about phylogenetic classification. Then we need techniques to detect phylogeny. The source of those techniques is our understanding of how traits change in evolution. The theory of evolution, therefore, not only guarantees the philosophy of classification: it is also the breeding ground of taxonomic techniques.

7 Why do Species exist?

Living things are classified into distinct units, called species: how can this practice be justified? Do species really exist as units in nature? Or are they merely divisions invented by taxonomists? These questions had been discussed by the philosophers of two millennia before the rise of Darwinism, for they are special cases of a wider philosophical question, that of why we classify anything at all. In biology, the question has been asked more often of species than any other category, perhaps because species are common-sense units in nature, such as chimpanzees, lions, wolves, robins, or herring. Two main answers have been offered, which in turn form two concepts of species: the realistic concept, according to which species exist as discrete units in nature, and the nominalistic (or artificial) concept, according to which they do not.

Such are the two possibilities. How are we to find out which is correct? Our method must be to decide first what the word species means, and then to examine nature to find out whether species in that sense exist in nature. If they do, species are real: if they do not, then the units we call species must be artificial.

What, then, does the word species mean? Biology recognizes two main meanings, which can be called the reproductive and the morphological (or phenetic) species concepts. According to the reproductive species concept, species are communities of interbreeding organisms; an individual belongs to the species whose members it can successfully reproduce with. Thus, one common definition of the species, due to Ernst Mayr, defines species as 'groups of actually or potentially interbreeding natural populations that are reproductively isolated from other such groups'. What we are here calling the reproductive species concept is also called (by its enthusiasts) the biological species concept, but that is a verbal vanity to be resisted, for the morphological concept is just as biological as the reproductive concept. According to the morphological concept, species are defined by their appearance. Individuals in nature, it would say, fall into discrete categories just by their set of phenotypes; the criterion of membership of a species on the morphological concept is to look sufficiently like other members of the species.

Real species exist in nature in both senses. It (probably) really is true, for example, that all humans can reproduce with all other humans and not with any other individuals. It might be possible, with techniques of sufficient sophistication, for a human and a chimp to produce a viable offspring; but this event is rare and unnatural enough to ignore in practice. An interbreeding community of individuals, the human species, does exist in nature. For the case of the reproductive concept therefore the realistic theory of species must be preferred to the nominalistic. If species were units artificially imposed on nature, as nominalism would require, then any living organism (of any species) should be able to interbreed with any other living organism of the opposite sex; or at least there should be a gradual change, as interbreeding became less and less efficient with more and more distantly related individuals. We have now seen that is not true in nature. Living organisms do occur in fairly discrete units, within which they can interbreed with almost equal efficiency, and outside which they can scarcely interbreed at all.

Real reproductive units exist in nature then; but so too do morphological units. Nominalism would suggest that the divisions of species are arbitrary lines drawn on a seamless continuum. This can be tested by physical measurement. It turns out that organisms in nature, at any one time and place, do come in relatively discrete arrays of physical forms, divided by at least statistically real gaps.

Anthropology provides further evidence. If species are artificial divisions, different independent classifications should recognize different species. Tribes with no knowledge of Western classifications should divide up living forms into different units from those of Western taxonomists. In fact they do not. The Kalam of New Guinea, for instance, recognize 174 species of vertebrates, all but four of which correspond to species recognized by Western taxonomists working on museum collections. The obvious explanation is that the species are in some sense real. In this case the sense is presumably morphological. Neither the museum taxonomist nor the local tribe is likely to have used the reproductive concept, because it is respectively too impractical or too sophisticated.

Species therefore are real, whether they are conceived as reproductive or morphological entities. But what of the higher taxonomic levels? Are the genus, the family, the order also real? Here the answer does depend on the distinction of reproductive and morphological concepts. The morphological concept could apply simultaneously to all levels of the classificatory hierarchy, but the reproductive concept can logically only apply to one. If species are distinguished by interbreeding, the higher levels of genus, family (and so on) cannot be as well; if the members of different species do not interbreed, then all the members of a genus cannot. For this reason, biologists who define species reproductively generally also argue that the species is the only real category in the taxonomic hierarchy, the others being relatively artificial conventions. However a morphological theory of real units can apply at several levels. Just as species are arrays of forms with statistical gaps between them, genera may be more inclusive arrays of forms, also divided by statistical gaps. Biologists who define species morphologically therefore more often also argue that the other levels of the hierarchy possess the same kind of reality as do species.

Because species have evolved from other species, the existence of discrete reproductive and morphological species is only true of the array of forms at any one time. Chimps and humans for instance are now separate species; but if we traced the continuous evolutionary series of their ancestors, the distinction would by degrees break down. We should eventually come to a time (perhaps five million years ago) when the ancestors formed a single population, chimp ancestors being neither reproductively nor morphologically distinguishable from human ancestors. The reality of any particular species is a temporary state of affairs; what is real now may not have been five million years ago, nor may it be five million years into the future. If, in order for species to count as real, they had *always* to be distinct from other species then species would not be real.

We can now understand why many evolutionary biologists of the nineteenth century, including Darwin, denied the reality of species. They had in mind a meaning of real that was timeless. If we consider the complete evolutionary continuum, species are artificial divisions. But those biologists would, I think, have agreed that species are real in the sense that we have used, which only refers to a particular time. Species are contingently real, the contingency being with respect to time. A similar argument could be made for space. In the continuous geographical variation of ring species (p. 6) for instance, species only really exist at a particular place.

But even at any one time, some species may be indistinguishable because they are just on the point of splitting into two. These must be admitted as unreal. However they are probably the exception rather than the rule. The number of species actually splitting at any one time is probably small because the rate of evolution relative to the human time-scale is slow. The majority of species will be reproductively and morphologically real.

We have now finished with the question of whether species really do exist: we must accept that they do. Let us now ask why. There are again two main ideas, which can be loosely, if not exactly, related to the reproductive and morphological species concepts. Associated with the reproductive species concept is the idea that species exist because their members interbreed among themselves but not with other species; the identity of species is due to what is called gene flow. When two individuals breed together genes flow from the two parents into their common offspring. With continual interbreeding among the individuals of a species, the genes of the species will (from generation to generation) be constantly circulating through its members. According to this theory, constant interbreeding and its resulting gene flow prevent the species from splitting up. Let us call this the gene-flow theory of species; according to it, species exist as morphological units only because they are interbreeding communities. We shall examine it further in a moment; but first let us state the other main idea. We shall call it the adaptive theory, and it states that species exist because only certain arrays of forms are adapted to the environment that they occupy. The resources of nature (the adaptive theory would suggest) exist in discrete zones—often called adaptive zones—each occupied by a species. Intermediates between species, being adapted to a gap between the zones of natural resources, would be eliminated by natural selection. There would be no resources to support them. According to the gene-flow theory, species are maintained by interbreeding; according to the adaptive theory, they are maintained by natural selection.

The two theories, as we shall see, need not be alternatives. But they have often been argued about as if they were. In order to understand the arguments, it is quite convenient to consider the adaptive and gene-flow theories, in an extreme form, as if they were competitors. We can put them together later. Let us return to the gene-flow theory, to ask exactly how it explains why species exist. Suppose that an array of interbreeding forms (a reproductive species) occupies a range of different environments. Suppose also that the exact form favoured by natural selection differs from place to place, as was the case, for example, for the peppered moth (p. 27). In that species, after the Industrial Revolution, the melanic type was favoured in industrial areas and the peppered type in unpolluted places. The melanic form increased in frequency where it was favoured.

Now, gene flow acts to reduce the divergence of a species in different places. As Mayr says, 'a population cannot change drastically as long as it is exposed to the normalizing effects of gene flow'. No biologist would disagree, except that the exact meaning of drastically might be open to argument. The question is whether it is a strong enough force to maintain the identity of species. According to the gene-flow theory, it is. Moreover, gene flow not only maintains species, but is the main factor doing so. Mayr, who is the main advocate of the gene-flow theory, believes 'the steady and high genetic input caused by gene flow is the main factor responsible for genetic cohesion among the populations of a species'. (Genetic cohesion means that the parts of a species are not diverging from one another.)

We can consider the exact mechanism in terms of the peppered moth. In an area where the black type was favoured, the genes encoding blackness increased in frequency every generation; where the peppered type was favoured, the genes for peppered coloration did. The frequencies of the genes would have begun to vary geographically, and the species to split. That is the effect of natural selection; but now for the effect of interbreeding. Because of migration of moths from one place to another and because natural selection would not be strong enough to eliminate all the bearers of a gene in one generation, both types would be present in any one place. If the moths mated indiscriminately with respect to colour (as peppered moths do) peppered and melanic types would interbreed. In a place where the melanic type was favoured, some peppered genes would be perpetuated in the off-spring of these matings. Interbreeding acts to reduce the divergence that is being favoured by natural selection. The gene flow among the regions of a species' range acts to standardize their gene frequencies.

The standardization of the species by gene flow will not be without effect on its adaptation. Instead of being perfectly adapted to each place, the species as a whole will come to possess a rough average adaptation which serves well across the whole range. The parts of the range where the species is relatively abundant will enjoy the most influence. More migrants will be sent out from that area, swamping other areas with the type adapted to the area of high abundance.

Mayr extends this argument to explain the relative stability of species' borders. If natural selection controlled the forms of species, he says, we should expect borders to extend gradually, as the individuals of the species' border, over the generations, adapt to their local conditions. But if the form of species is controlled by gene flow, we should expect the rare forms at the border to be swamped by the more numerous migrants from the centre of the range. The species would be incapable of adjusting to the conditions at the border. It would be best adapted to the conditions at the centre of its range and gradually worse and worse adapted to the conditions towards the periphery. At some point, the level of adaptation would approach zero; that would be the border. It is in fact not known whether species' borders are stable, because the rate of evolution is too slow relative to human life-scale. But even if they are, it would not be strong evidence for the gene-flow theory, because the stability of species' borders can also be explained by natural selection. But the idea, whatever its validity, does illustrate the gene-flow theory in action.

The adaptive theory, in its extreme form, denies that inter-breeding maintains species. It explains the existence of discrete natural species by natural selection. Species are adapted to the resources that they live on. If the resources of nature form discontinuous zones, natural selection will give rise to discontinuous species exploiting them. If the resources are continuously distributed, natural selection will act to produce continuous variation in the species, to match their resources. Continuous variation is common in nature. It is usually seen along a geographic gradient, in which case it is called a cline. Clines are usually of rather limited extent; the extreme usually represent no more than a sub-specific level of difference, presumably because resources only vary continuously over a small scale.

In fact very little is known about the variation of resources in nature or, for that matter, about exactly how natural selection operates in relation to particular patterns of resource variation. Natural selection would not usually produce discrete species when the distribution of resources is continuous; but in some special circumstances it can. The adaptive theory might either assume that the special circumstances are so rare that they can be ignored, or it might argue backwards from the fact that species do often exist as discrete units to the hypothetical explanation that they represent adaptations to a discrete distribution of resources. Either way, the theory stands by its explanation of species. The adaptive theory, let me add, is embodied in what is sometimes called the evolutionary species concept, which has been defined by G. G. Simpson as 'a lineage (an ancestral–descendant sequence of populations) evolving separately from others and with its own evolutionary role and tendencies'.

Now that we have defined the two theories we must try to find out which is more correct. They are meant to explain why species exist; they both pass this test, for both the reproductive and morphological meanings of species. Indeed, the two theories would in their different ways subsume the morphological and reproductive concepts in a single factor. The gene-flow theory explains the morphological pattern by interbreeding, which makes the morphological concept superfluous. The pattern of interbreeding is the fundamental variable.

In the adaptive theory, the morphological and reproductive concepts are both explained by one factor, natural selection. The pattern of morphology, as we have seen, it explains by adaptation to resource zones. How does it deal with the pattern of interbreeding? There is no difficulty. The reproductive species concept means that individuals choose to mate with other individuals that are relatively like themselves. Now, natural selection can work on reproductive behaviour as well as any other trait. The reproductive behaviour of the fruitfly *Drosophila* for instance has been altered by artificial selection. Natural selection will ensure that individuals so choose their mates that they produce the best possible offspring. If genes regularly flow by immigration into an area that they are not well adapted to, natural selection would act to prevent the locals from mating with the immigrants. Locals who mated with other locals would leave better-adapted offspring than locals who mated indiscriminately. By this means, natural selection will make good reproductive species. The reproductive species concept can thus be incorporated in the adaptive theory of species.

The two theories agree that the reproductive and morphological aspects of species are real and correlated. But for the correlation they offer different causal explanations. In the gene-flow theory, the pattern of reproduction is the cause and the pattern of morphological adaptation is the effect. In the adaptive theory the causal arrow is reversed. Natural selection favours a pattern of morphological adaptation, and the pattern of interbreeding is thought to be adjusted (also by natural selection) to fit the favoured morphological pattern. Because the reproductive and morphological aspects are closely correlated in nature, no general test is possible between the two theories. Fortunately the natural correlation is not perfect. There are a few cases in which natural selection and gene flow favour different morphological patterns, and in them we can see which factor is more powerful. The result may suggest which variable is the cause of the usually inextricable correlation of interbreeding and morphological adaptation.

We are after two kinds of test case. One is where there is gene flow but natural selection favours divergence; the other is where there is no gene flow but natural selection favours uniformity. The predictions of the two theories are diametrically opposed. The gene-flow theory predicts that divergence cannot take place in the face of gene flow; the adaptive theory predicts that it can. The gene-flow theory predicts that uniformity in different places requires gene flow between them; the adaptive theory predicts that natural selection alone can produce it. That is the principle of the test. Let us now try to apply it.

The mining industry in Great Britain has thrown up large slag heaps of waste material from beneath the ground. The slag heaps have, in many cases, high concentrations of such metals as copper, lead, and tin, which prevent the growth of ordinary plants. The slag heaps are left barren and ugly. But some odd patches of grasses, such as the species *Agrostis tenuis*, do manage to grow. *A. tenuis* grows in normal environments as well, and experiments (mainly by A. D. Bradshaw and his colleagues) have shown that there are two types of the grass. The type that grows on slag heaps is more tolerant of metals in its substrate than are normal members of the same species. The higher tolerance, as breeding experiments reveal, is due to a genetic difference from the ordinary grass.

There is clearly strong selection for divergence. On the slag heaps only the tolerant grasses can survive; but on the surrounding ground tolerance to high metals is not needed (and is even selected against). The selection pressure is effective, for there is rapid divergence. The rate of the divergence differs on the upwind and the downwind side of the slag heap, but is high on both sides. It takes place over about 150 yards on the downwind side, and over only a yard or two on the upwind side—within a few paces the type of *Agrostis tenuis* changes completely from tolerant to intolerant. We have now established the action of natural selection and the pattern of morphology, but what about the third factor of interest, the amount of gene flow? It is immense. Pollen blows back and forth over that narrow interval where the grasses are varying from metal-tolerant to normal. At least in the case of *A. tenuis* on slag heaps, gene flow has not prevented extreme divergence favoured by natural selection. The difference between the rate of divergence upwind and downwind shows that the amount of gene flow is not irrelevant, however. There is also some sign that natural selection is acting to bring about speciation between the metal-tolerant and intolerant types of *A. tenuis*. The two types flower at different average times and self-fertilize to some extent, which factors will both act to reduce the amount of interbreeding. But although it is reduced, it is not prevented; the two types still belong in the same reproductive species.

The adaptive theory comes out slightly better from the case of *Agrostis*; but there can be no doubt that gene flow is powerful enough to restrain, if too weak to prevent, divergence. Let us now turn to the other test case. Where there is no interbreeding, does the morphological pattern diverge? The clearest evidence comes from asexual species. If the adaptive theory is correct asexual organisms should form species just like sexual organisms, for natural selection works on both. If the gene-flow theory is correct asexual organisms should not form discrete species like those of their sexual relatives. Such are the opposed predictions: the facts unambiguously favour the adaptive theory. Asexual organisms form recognizable morphological units just like sexual species.

We can consider the same test case in a sexual species. *Cepaea nemoralis* is a small sexually reproducing land snail, coloured by a number of bands on its shell. It lives in most regions of Europe, including the Pyrenees, where a study relevant to our purpose has been conducted by Steve Jones and his colleagues. *Cepaea* occupies relative lowlands: it is rarely found at heights above 1,500m and never above 2,000m. It lives in the river valleys, separated by the mountains between. Most river valley populations are therefore isolated from other such populations; and we can be reasonably certain there is no gene flow between them. The snails show variation both in their proteins and in the colour pattern of their shells.

The crucial question is whether the populations in different river valleys are uniform or have diverged from each other. For the shell pattern, the answer is simple: they are uniform; the frequencies of different shell types are much the same in all populations. For protein polymorphism, it is slightly more complex. The frequencies of different protein forms have diverged in different areas, but into a pattern that transcends the mountainous barriers to gene flow. Three main areas can be recognized by the kinds of proteins that they have in high frequency, but within each of the three areas there are several river valleys separated by mountains. The uniformity within the three areas cannot only be due to gene flow.

Both shell types and proteins tell the same story. Different populations, with no gene flow between them, can remain uniform. This fact contradicts the gene-flow theory of why species exist. It fits the adaptive theory. The fit however is only at an abstract level; it is not a strong confirmation. In order to confirm the adaptive theory, we should have to work out how natural selection affects the shell types and the proteins, and then determine whether the force of natural selection is the same in the river valleys with similar *Cepaea* populations. Practically nothing is known about how natural selection operates on the protein polymorphisms of *Cepaea*. Rather a lot is known about the action of natural selection on the shell patterns. But although much is known, it adds up to a confusing story. Many factors—predation by birds and several climatic ones—have been shown to select for particular shell patterns. Lighter-coloured shells (Jones has shown) enjoy an advantage where the sunlight is stronger. The patterns of spatial variation in shell coloration in the Pyrenees may be caused by the patterns of intensity of sunlight, for different places with the same sunlight do seem to have snails of the same colour. But although this may be the true explanation it has not yet been confirmed in sufficient detail for confident conclusions to be drawn.

The adaptive theory is favoured by both examples. And both *Agrostis* and the *Cepaea* of the Pyrenees were only illustrative examples. They must stand for many others. An enthusiast of the gene-flow theory of species could perhaps poke holes in each one in turn; but it is difficult to believe that natural selection does not operate in any of them. And yet, although the facts might appear to favour the adaptive over the gene-flow theory, we should not conclude that the adaptive theory is correct and the gene-flow theory incorrect. That would be unwise not only because the tests so far are imperfect, but also because in nature the dichotomy of gene flow and natural selection is probably often false. Let us finish by examining this point.

What is the relation of gene flow and natural selection? They can oppose each other in the manner we have discussed. But they may often not. If natural selection could adjust the level of gene flow to fit the pattern of morphological adaptation, they would not oppose each other. Moreover, natural selection probably can so adjust the level of gene flow by its effect on mate choice. I say probably because it cannot be proved by any facts at present, and at least one authority, Mayr, denies it; but a reasonably logical case can be made. We can use the grass *A. tenuis* as an example. In that species, interbreeding between metal-tolerant and metal-intolerant forms must produce, each generation, a large number of non-adaptive types: metal-intolerant *A. tenuis* on the slag heap and metal-tolerant *A. tenuis* off it. We in fact know that cross-breeding in this case has been reduced below the maximum possible. But let us suppose, for sake of argument, that it had not. Let us suppose that the two forms interbred indiscriminately. If they did, natural selection would favour a more discriminate choice of reproductive partner. We need only compare the success of a hypothetically undiscriminating *A. tenuis* with that of a hypothetical *A. tenuis* that crossed with its own type (that is, metal-tolerant with metal-tolerant and metal-intolerant with metal-intolerant, but not tolerant with intolerant). The undiscriminating *A. tenuis* produce many offspring that are not adapted to their substrate, whereas most of the offspring of the choosy *A. tenuis* would be properly adapted. The choosy *A. tenuis* would leave more surviving offspring, and be favoured by natural selection. The level of gene flow would be reduced.

One should then ask why the two forms of *Agrostis* interbreed at all. It seems they would do better not to. (This kind of fact is part of the reason why such authorities as Mayr deny that natural selection can adjust the level of gene flow in the manner we have just discussed.) There are several possible answers. One is that they continue to interbreed because, for some reason, natural selection is incapable of reducing the level of interbreeding. Quite why it should be so paralysed we cannot say, although we could invoke the constraints discussed in Chapter 4. Another answer might be that natural selection slowly is reducing the level of gene flow, but there has not yet been enough time for it to reach zero. After all, slag heaps are a relatively recent introduction to the environment of *Agrostis*, and it takes some time for natural selection to adjust a population to an environmental change. A third possible answer is that, for some unknown reason, it is best for *Agrostis* to have an intermediate level of gene flow (as it does have), below the maximum but above zero. We do not know which of these answers is correct. The fact that interbreeding has been reduced to some extent suggests that natural selection is not wholly powerless; it may even be in control.

If we accept that, in cases like *Agrostis tenuis*, natural selection can adjust the level of interbreeding to the locally adaptive level, then natural selection and gene flow are not opposite factors. Their opposition can only be temporary in evolutionary time and inconsequential in evolutionary effect, for whenever they are opposed natural selection will set to work to adjust the amount of interbreeding.

It has only been possible to make a consistent story out of weak tests and poorly confirmed theories. The problem can only be satisfactorily resolved by more exact observation. Levels of gene flow and forces of natural selection are both, although sometimes only with difficulty, measurable. The extent to which the uniformity of species is caused by gene flow and selection could then be determined quantitatively. The extremes of the adaptive and gene-flow theories would be replaced by quantitative degrees. That is how they must be in nature. Both gene flow and natural selection do undoubtedly operate between populations; both must affect gene frequencies. The problem is whether one is more important. At present we can only draw our conclusions from uncertain arguments and inexact observations; but evidence and probability do now suggest that the uniformity and divergence of populations is mainly controlled by natural selection.

8 How can One Species split into Two?

If the modern species of plants and animals have all evolved from a single common ancestor, ancestral species must on millions of occasions have split into two or more descendent species. The process of splitting is called speciation, and it raises two general questions: under what circumstances does speciation take place, and what is the exact nature of the event? The questions are not wholly separate, but for our purposes they must be replaced by five more specific ones. Taking the questions of circumstances first, we shall ask whether speciation takes place only when a species becomes geographically divided; and whether the populations leading to the formation of new species are especially small. Then, concerning the nature of the event, we shall ask whether the amount of genetic change at speciation is large or small; and whether the change is adaptive or random in direction. We shall finish by asking whether speciation requires any special kinds of genetic changes.

Speciation is a process of great importance in evolution. It results not only in the formation of new species, but of all higher groups as well. After enough rounds of speciation, sufficiently different forms will be produced to be classified in new genera, families, and so on. Whatever processes have caused speciation have probably also been responsible for the origin of higher groups too. The study of speciation is also a way of asking about the importance of natural selection in evolution. We have established that natural selection is the cause of adaptation. But is it the cause of all evolution? If it is, it must be the main driving force behind speciation. If we are to establish the scope of natural selection, we must understand the mechanism of speciation.

The five particular questions we shall consider are suggested by what is often called the peripheral isolate model of speciation.

This model, which has been most ably defended by Ernst Mayr, gives unambiguous answers to four of the five. It has been widely influential, so much so indeed that some biologists are unaware it is controversial. According to the peripheral isolate model, speciation takes place by rapid evolution in small populations geographically isolated from the main population of the species. The genetic changes at speciation (it supposes) are large, so large as to amount to a whole 'genetic revolution'; they may also be in high proportion random rather than driven by natural selection. We shall examine the reasons behind the model as we proceed; but for now we only need to know that the model exists and is influential, and what answers it offers to those five questions. Then we can order this chapter as a critical examination of the peripheral isolate model of speciation.

But first we must define speciation. Clearly, it is the evolution of a new species, but that re-raises the problem of what a species is. As we saw in the last chapter, there are two main criteria, reproductive and morphological. We also saw that in most cases in nature the two properties are mixed. Let us therefore also mix them in our definition. Let us define speciation as the evolution of a new discrete morphological array of forms that interbreed only among themselves.

Definition is not very important here, for we shall not be trying to judge whether particular instances should be counted as speciation. We shall take such facts as there are for granted, and use them to judge ideas. The first set of ideas, which have dominated twentieth-century discussions of speciation, concern geography. The question is whether speciation only takes place when a species is split into geographically isolated populations. According to the allopatric (other place) theory, it does, and according to the sympatric (same place) theory it does not. I shall first describe the two theories and then ask which (if either) is correct.

Speciation, in the allopatric theory, takes place as follows. To start with there is only one species with a continuous geographic distribution. Then, for some reason, some of its members become geographically isolated from the rest of the species, perhaps because a river cuts through the former continuous range of a land-dwelling species or a bridge of land separates a formerly continuous stretch of water. New rivers and land bridges are rare events, however, and the movements of the organisms themselves may be a commoner cause of geographical separation: a few individuals may incidentally be isolated after migrating together far away from the normal geographic range of the species. But whatever the reason, a continuous population must be split. The next stage of allopatric speciation is for the two populations to undergo different evolutionary changes in their different environments: they diverge. If they diverge enough, the two populations may be classified as different geographic races, and then as different species.

At any point the geographic ranges of the populations may again change. The geographically separated populations may move together, and their individual members mingle and meet. What will happen now probably depends on how much the two populations have evolved apart. If they are still much the same, their members may mate together and the two populations simply fuse to become a single population again. But if they have become very different, they might not be able to interbreed; the two populations would then have become two species.

Such is the theory of allopatric speciation. According to the sympatric theory, much the same process of divergence can take place without the geographical separation of the populations. The first stage is for natural selection to favour the evolution of two forms within the continuous range of a species. If the force of natural selection is strong enough, two forms could evolve in the face of interbreeding (as happened, for instance, in *Agrostis tenuis* on slag heaps, see p. 97). If the process continued far enough the two forms might diverge sufficiently to look like different species. If the offspring of crosses between individuals of the same form survived better than the offspring of crosses between the different forms, natural selection would favour a reduction of interbreeding between the two forms. Speciation would then result from divergence followed by selection to reduce interbreeding.

A third kind of speciation, intermediate between the two extremes, is called parapatric (or semi-geographic) speciation. In this form, the divergence takes place between contiguous, rather than separated or overlapping, populations. We shall not discuss

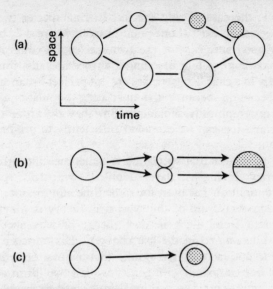

Fig. 7. Three modes of speciation.
Time proceeds to the right, space is represented up the page; shading indicates the formation of a new species. (a) allopatric (b) parapatric (c) sympatric. The spatial area occupied by a species is referred to in the text as the species' 'range'.

parapatric speciation separately, because the arguments for and against it are much the same as for sympatric speciation. In covering sympatric we shall cover most of the main arguments about parapatric speciation. The three kinds of speciation are illustrated in Figure 7.

In their attitudes to these models, evolutionary biologists divide into two main camps. Some maintain that almost all speciation is allopatric, and others that speciation is at least sometimes sympatric or parapatric. Although other positions are logically possible, no one in practice holds them. No one denies that at least some cases of speciation have been allopatric. The question at issue is whether all or merely some speciation is allopatric, and likewise whether some or no speciation is sympatric.

Allopatric speciation is both coherent in theory and well supported in fact. We have already met the clearest evidence in

Chapter 1, the case of ring species. In ring species two closely related species co-exist at one point in space where they behave as perfectly good species, but the two species are connected by a continuous range of interbreeding intermediates distributed geographically in a ring. Ring species are not perfect instances of allopatric speciation because the speciating populations are not actually geographically separated. But they do prove that geographic variation can be extended sufficiently to produce speciation.

If no one doubts that speciation is sometimes allopatric, many evolutionary biologists have doubted sympatric speciation. Indeed, to doubt it has been for some time almost an orthodoxy. The best-known critic of the sympatric theory is Mayr, whose doubts stem from the gene-flow theory of why species exist (which we examined in the last chapter). His criticism is argumentative, not factual. He thinks that natural selection is so feeble a force compared with gene flow that two forms could not evolve in sympatry. The continual interbreeding between them would prevent divergence. Divergence would only be possible if the two forms become reproductively isolated. That however is not possible in sympatry. The 'isolation mechanism' (that is, the mechanism to prevent interbreeding) would have to arise and be established by natural selection in an impossibly short interval of time, while the two forms co-existed in the population. If there ever were two forms it could only be for a brief interval before their interbreeding fused them into a single type. The sympatric theory, according to Mayr, is inescapably paradoxical. The stable co-existence of two forms is not possible without reproductive isolation; but reproductive isolation cannot evolve unless the two forms stably co-exist. This of course is an entirely theoretical argument, and it may not be valid. Perhaps natural selection can be powerful enough to cause the divergence and stable co-existence of two forms without reproductive isolation. Isolating mechanisms could then take their time to evolve later. While argument and evidence remain unpersuasive it is not unreasonable to believe that isolating mechanisms may evolve under natural selection in sympatry. Sympatric speciation cannot be ruled out in theory.

Let us now consider an example. It is of two species of those attractive insects called lacewings. The two in particular live in North America and are called *Chrysopa carnea* and *C. downesi*; they have been studied by C. J. Tauber and M. J. Tauber. They behave in nature as two species: they look different, *carnea* being light green in the spring and summer and changing to brown in autumn and *downesi* being dark green all year; they live in different places, *carnea* occupying grasslands, meadows, and deciduous trees, *downesi* living only on conifers (the two species therefore are camouflaged against their different backgrounds); and they breed at different times, *carnea* in the winter and again in the summer, *downesi* only once in the spring. No hybrids between the two species are found in nature.

However, when the two species are put together in the laboratory, and deceived as to the time of year, they mate and produce fertile offspring. Tauber and Tauber took advantage of this exceptional state of affairs to study the genetics of the differences between the species. They found that the species differ for only three sets of genes. One of the three controls colour. It has two alleles which we can call G_1 and G_2: G_1G_1 produces a dark green colour and is the genotype of *downesi*; G_2G_2 produces the light green colour of *carnea*; and G_1G_2 produces an intermediate— neither allele is dominant—that is never seen in nature. The other two genes control when the lacewing breeds. The genes actually exert their control through the photoperiod response. Lacewings, like many species, time their breeding by daylength (called the photoperiod). Again there are two alleles of each gene; but this time in both genes one of the alleles is dominant to the other. A lacewing with two recessive alleles of each gene behaves like *downesi*, and is ready to breed in the spring; a lacewing with at least one dominant allele breeds at the same time as *carnea*.

The geographic range of *downesi* is completely within that of *carnea*, and (the Taubers say) there is no evidence that either has ever been isolated from the other. They suggest instead that the lacewings split sympatrically. They suggest that the colour poly- morphism arose first, with dark green individuals living on con- ifers and light green ones on deciduous plants and grass. This would have been divergence in sympatry, in the face of gene flow;

but we have met other examples of it and know that it can occur. We also know that there would have been a continual production of inferior heterozygotes of intermediate colour, camouflaged neither to conifers nor non-conifers. A reduction of interbreeding would be advantageous. Any change that reduced interbreeding (and did not cause any other disruption) would be favoured by natural selection. The first such change to arise (the Taubers suggest) was the mutation altering the photoperiodic response, which caused the different lacewings to breed at different times. It is an effective method of reducing interbreeding. Thus two changes in three genes were enough to cause sympatric speciation in *Chrysopa*.

Partisans of the theory of allopatric speciation might say that the isolation of the two *Chrysopa* by breeding season is 'really' equivalent to allopatric isolation, and that this is therefore 'really' a form of allopatric speciation. In a sense, isolation by breeding season is analogous to isolation by geography, but there is the important difference that the isolation is sympatric. Whenever there is speciation, there must be isolation between the two speciating forms: that is required by definition. If all kinds of isolation were said to be 'really' allopatric whether or not they really were, then the case for allopatric speciation will be won by an act of definition. The most sensible position is to define allopatry and sympatry, as in Figure 7 above, by geography. If the species splits within its continuous range, then speciation is sympatric. The speciation of *Chrysopa* (if the Taubers' model is correct) really was sympatric.

Reasonably certain examples exist of both sympatric and allopatric speciation. We have now covered one of each. But, as so often in evolutionary biology, the difficult problem is not whether a process works, but how common it is in nature. Is allopatric, parapatric, or sympatric speciation the more common? Enough cases have not been studied to prove, by factual enumeration, whether one is commoner than the others: each study takes too long. In the absence of direct evidence, we have to fall back on less direct arguments concerning the inherent plausibility of the processes, or on indirect evidence. Both have been put forward in favour of the theory of allopatric speciation.

An argument from inherent plausibility we have already met. It works against the theory of sympatric speciation. Natural selection for divergence (it says) is too weak to overcome standardization by gene flow. Gene flow certainly can act to reduce divergence; but whether it is powerful enough to prevent it in the face of natural selection is another matter. The material of the previous chapter, and the instance of *Chrysopa*, are enough to show that divergence despite interbreeding is at least possible. Argument therefore is no guide; but what about indirect evidence? The facts of geographic variation have often been cited in favour of the theory of allopatric speciation. It has been proved at length—and we are not going to work through the proof here—that all the facts of geographic variation and distribution can be explained by the theory of allopatric speciation. One need only invoke divergence in isolation and subsequent changes in geographic range, and any facts can be explained. The proof however is not evidence in favour of the theory of allopatric speciation. Just as the allopatric theory can account for all the facts, so too can the other two theories. Sympatric or parapatric speciation followed by changes in geographic range could also account for all the facts of geographic variation and distribution. They cannot be used to choose among the theories. It is impossible to conclude whether one of the processes of speciation is commoner. The problem is unresolved.

Let us turn now from the geography to the size of speciating populations. Are they large or small: do they contain many or few individuals? Although we do not need an exact criterion of what counts as a large and what as a small population, they might be roughly distinguished as follows. The population sizes of species differ enormously; but in many cases they are of the order of thousands to tens of thousands. If the population size of a species were 10,000, and the species then split into two, then the speciating population would be 'large' if it was anywhere near 5,000 (say, if it were more than 1,000) and 'small' if it were less than, say, about 50. These are merely approximate and informal figures.

What facts do we possess? Whatever they are, they are likely to be unconvincing, because speciation itself cannot easily be observed—in most cases it took place in the past. There may be evidence from the fossil record, and perhaps some other kinds of indirect evidence. Let us look at one case of each. The fossil record is not much help with detailed questions about such geologically rapid processes as speciation. The record is usually not complete enough. We can however consider one exceptionally detailed study. It concerns snails, living about one to five million years ago, in Lake Turkana (East Kenya); the work was done by P. G. Williamson. In the samples studied by Williamson, speciation appears to have taken place several times. (This is controversial. Large changes can be induced in snails merely by bringing them up in different environments. The changes observed by Williamson, and attributed to speciation, are similar in nature and degree to environmentally induced changes. Some experts suspect that Williamson's observations are not of speciation. But, with appropriate caution, we shall follow Williamson here.)

The fossil record studied by Williamson was sufficiently complete that he could roughly estimate the population size of the speciating populations. They were very large, containing (as he wrote) 'many millions of individuals'. This one controversial fossil study does not suggest that speciating populations are small; but it is hardly conclusive.

A second kind of evidence is much less direct. It uses, as an indirect estimate of population size, the geographic range of the species: the two are perhaps approximately correlated. It indirectly selects speciating populations by comparing the ranges of pairs of species that have recently split from a common ancestor: one of the pair has probably recently split off from the other. The advantage is that these facts are known for many species. Population sizes themselves are rarely measured; but geographic ranges often are. Speciation itself can rarely be seen, but we do know, for some groups, which pairs of species are most closely related. A conclusion can therefore be drawn for a large sample. Sydney Anderson and Mary Evensen for instance examined the relationships and geographic ranges of all the species of North American vertebrates. They reasoned that if speciating populations are small, one of a pair of closely related species should have a much smaller range than the other. The argument is tenuous;

but their conclusion is perhaps of interest. In fact, both species in each pair usually had rather similar range sizes. 'More than half the recently divergent pairs have the range of the smaller species greater than 30 per cent of that of the larger species'. More than 30 per cent is not remarkably small. This indirect evidence suggests that speciating populations may be about the same size as non-speciating populations.

The evidence concerning the size of speciating populations is indirect and unconvincing. It is worth mentioning, however, just to show that confident conclusions are completely inappropriate. The problem is difficult to solve. But such evidence as there is, I think, suggests that speciating populations are not especially small.

Now that we have seen the quality of the evidence we might wonder how anyone ever dared to argue that speciating populations are small. They cannot have been compelled or even tantalized by facts, for there are hardly any facts at all and these are too fragile to support any conclusion. The explanation is that it was the conclusion not of observation but of reason. The small size of speciating populations was thought to be needed to account for other properties of speciation. The whole idea was this. Species (it was suggested) differ for a large number of genes. (The arguments why this is so are involved and inconclusive and best ignored here: let us accept it for sake of argument.) The large genetic differences, in turn, were believed mainly to arise during speciation, which entails a 'genetic revolution'. Natural selection, it was thought, working a gene at a time, would be too slow and feeble a force to bring about a genetic revolution. Some more extreme circumstance would be needed. The proposed revolutionary situation was a small isolated population. Here (it was thought) evolution would be more rapid than in a large population. Moreover, random changes were thought to be capable of effecting what natural selection could not—a genetic revolution—and random processes are more powerful in small populations than in large. The small size of speciating populations, in short, was postulated to produce two of the effects required in the peripheral isolate model: rapid evolution and random evolution.

The next stage must be to examine the theory itself of the genetic revolution. The question of the rate of evolution in small populations we shall defer until the next chapter. Here, we shall concentrate (in this order) on whether reason and evidence demonstrate large genetic differences between species, large genetic changes at speciation (as opposed to any other time), and random evolution in small populations. As we do so we can keep the question of the size of speciating populations in mind. The fossil and indirect evidence (as we have seen) was not compelling, but we may yet be led back to the conclusion that speciating populations are small if all the factual and theoretical postulates of the theory just outlined prove correct. Let us see whether they are.

Before we can say whether the genetic changes at speciation are large or small we shall need some approximate and informal criterion of a large and a small change. There are about 5,000 to 10,000 genetic loci in the genome of an animal. If only about (say) less than 50 of them changed at speciation, that could hardly count as a revolution; we could count that as a small change: but if there were changes at many hundred, perhaps a thousand, genes, that would be more like a large change.

Let us begin by settling a point of principle. New species do not *have* to evolve in a genetic revolution. If species are defined reproductively a new species can evolve by only a tiny genetic change: a single mutation (which must find its way into at least two individuals), that prevented interbreeding between the mutant and the ancestral types. A change in only one gene could achieve that in theory; but the change must be favoured by natural selection for it to be established in nature. The mutant and ancestral types must therefore also differ in some other respect, on account of which natural selection can favour the reduction in interbreeding. The two types must differ in at least two genes, one controlling interbreeding and the other some other difference for which a reduction in interbreeding would be advantageous. In principle, then, speciation can result from genetic changes at only two genes.

Moreover, it is not only a point of principle. It can be illustrated by evidence. We have considered the genetics of speciation in one case, the lacewings *Chrysopa. Chrysopa carnea* and *C. downesi* differ in only three genes, and changes at only two of them effected the complete production of a new species. There was no genetic revolution. In *Chrysopa*, the genetic change that produced a new species was in a gene (or two) controlling the photoperiodic response. But many other kinds of minor changes could produce the same result. A change in courtship, in the kind of preferred mate, in the place of breeding, could all reduce the amount of interbreeding within a former species.

Although the instance of *Chrysopa* does demonstrate that changes in many genes are not necessary for the evolution of a new species, it may not tell us the normal number of genetic changes on such occasions. *Chrysopa* is only one case, which may be exceptional. Single instances may illustrate general rules, but they cannot prove them. What is true of *Chrysopa* may not be true of other species. So, now that we have solved the problem of principle, if we are to tackle the general problem of fact we must move on to some other class of more abundant evidence.

The only conclusive evidence must concern genetic changes that took place at speciation. Unfortunately, this kind of evidence is very difficult to obtain. There is one copious source of evidence that bears on the problem, although it is too indirect to solve it finally. It is the evidence from the gel electrophoresis of proteins. This method (as we have seen) has been used to measure gene frequencies at large numbers of genes. If we are to work with gene frequencies, we shall need a more complex measure of genetic difference than the number of genes in which species differ. There are degrees of difference. When we compare a gene which has two alleles in two species, it is important to distinguish the case where alleles A and a are in proportions 0.9 and 0.1 in one species and 0.1 and 0.9 in the other from the case in which the proportions are 0.49 and 0.51 in one and 0.51 and 0.49 in the other. In both cases the species differ, but the difference is much greater in the former case. The difference can be measured for each allele as a 'distance' (for A in the former case the distance is $0.9 - 0.1 = 0.8$, in the second case $0.51 - 0.49 = 0.02$), which can be averaged for all the genes studied to give a measure of genetic distance.

Gel electrophoresis is a source of a large amount of reasonably representative evidence. It gives a reasonable estimate of the

Table 1 Genetic identities between species in various groups

Group	Identity among	
	local populations	species
Drosophila (fruitfly)	0.97	0.35, 0.56*
Lepomis (fish)	0.97	0.54
Anolis Bimini group (lizards)	0.97	0.21
Anolis rocquet group (lizards)	0.99	0.67
Thomomys (mammals)	0.93	0.85
Sigmodon (mammals)	0.98	0.76
Lupinus (lupin)	0.96	0.35
Stephanomeria (Compositae)	0.98	0.95

The identities are averages for many genes (the number differs between groups). Identity can vary from 0 to 1; when it is 1 the two populations are genetically identical.

Selected, and simplified, from several sources.

* (for *Drosophila*) identities for subspecies and semispecies within the *D. willistoni* group respectively.

average genetic difference between two species. But because genetic changes can (at least in theory) accumulate before and after, as well as at, speciation, the gel electrophoretic comparison does not reveal how much of the difference arose at speciation. It does, however, place an upper limit on the amount of genetic change at speciation. The genetic change at speciation cannot have exceeded the total difference between the two species (although it may of course have been much less). The evidence of gel electrophoresis can be used to test the theory of genetic revolution, but the test will be one-sided: the theory could be refuted but not confirmed. If the differences between species are consistently large, the evidence would not count for or against the theory; but if they are often small, the theory of genetic revolution would have to be rejected.

I have assembled, and simplified, a selection of the evidence in Table 1. (It is expressed as genetic identity, rather than genetic distance; identity is simply the inverse of distance: the higher the identity, the more similar are the gene frequencies.) The appropriate conclusion is that the evidence does not suggest anything in particular. The genetic differences between some species are large, between others they are small. If the differences between species are only about the same as between two populations of a species, they can be counted as small: as the Table shows, all degrees of distance, from this upwards, are found. In some cases, there may have been something approaching a genetic revolution, in other cases there may not.

Genetic revolutions are unnecessary in principle, and their frequency in fact cannot be determined with existing evidence. The first premise of the peripheral isolate model of speciation is therefore unconfirmed. And if the premise is shaky, the whole edifice including the postulated small size of speciating populations, becomes unreliable. But we can still examine the remaining postulate of the model, that random processes become effective in the hypothetical small speciating populations. Natural selection was therefore thought to be relatively unimportant in speciation, and the evolution of new species to be driven by a different kind of process from evolution within species.

Do random processes become effective against natural selection in small populations? The question is as much theoretical as observational, and before it can be answered must be posed in mathematical form. Thus, if a sample of n individuals is taken from a total population of N individuals, and if a gene has two alleles in the large population with frequencies p and $(1-p)$, what is the probability that the sample will have any given gene frequency? Obviously the most likely gene frequencies in the sample are p of the one allele and $(1-p)$ of the other; but there is also a chance that the sample may have different frequencies.

The mathematics is known exactly, but we need not work through it here. We only need to notice one general conclusion. The sample has to be very small indeed if there is to be much chance of the loss of an allele. For chance sampling to have much evolutionary effect, alleles must be completely lost. If their frequencies are merely altered, natural selection can soon restore them to their former values; but if an allele is actually lost, natural selection (until the allele reappears by mutation) cannot make it up again. If the sample contains only one individual, and it is a homozygote, all the alleles of the original population, except that one, will be lost. But this is an extreme case. It is unlikely that tiny populations, of only one or two individuals, are of much evolutionary importance, because they are unlikely to survive. If its one or two members are killed, the population is extinct. Larger populations are less likely to be killed off by the accidental death of individuals. But if the sample contains more than a tiny number of individuals, it will probably contain all the alleles of the original population (even exceptionally variable genes only have thirty or forty alleles in a population). We may conclude, then, theoretically, that the random sampling of genes during speciation is probably unimportant. Natural selection remains in control.

Our examination of the peripheral isolate model of speciation is now complete. We can deliver a general judgement on it. Its account of the geography of speciation has some reasonable, if not exclusive, generality. But its account of the population genetics of speciation is much less trustworthy. It is supported by neither reason nor evidence. There is no evidence that speciating populations are small; random sampling is a feeble force as opposed to natural selection even in tiny populations; large genetic changes are unnecessary in theory and at least sometimes unobserved in fact. To state the conclusions in more positive form, we may say that natural selection is probably the driving force of speciation, and that a narrow generalization concerning the amounts of genetic change and the size of populations at speciation would be inappropriate, for they probably vary widely from case to case.

We may finish with one more question about the genetics of speciation. So far we have asked about the extent of genetic change at speciation; we can now ask about their nature. Is any specific *kind* of genetic change characteristic of speciation? One answer must be true by definition. Genes controlling interbreeding must change at speciation. But what of other genes? Are any genes other than those controlling interbreeding associated with speciation? If there are, they will probably be genes for which interbreeding between the alternative forms is disadvantageous. Changes in such genes (if any exist) would precipitate speciation.

They would be genes of particular importance in speciation, which we might call speciation genes. Now, from time to time, various evolutionary biologists have suggested that speciation genes do exist. The most radical version of the idea is that evolution within a species concerns one set of genes, and evolution at speciation a quite different set. The main tradition in twentieth-century evolutionary biology has denied that any such separate set of speciation genes exists, but the heresy has had many supporters. The main reason for supposing that there are no special speciation genes is that variation can be found within species for all the same kinds of things that vary between species. A true speciation gene should only differ between species; it should be invariant within each species, because whenever a variant of it arises there is selection for it to form a new species. No such genes have ever been identified. The theory of speciation genes lacks factual support.

Chromosomal changes are one kind of genetic change that it is not heretical to suggest are important in speciation. The main observation which (it has been suggested) supports such a role is that the chromosomes of different species look different. Chromosomes can be seen down a microscope; they have a clear structure, of shape, size, and pattern of bands. This structure characteristically differs between species. It has been suggested that chromosomes differ between species because chromosomal changes cause speciation. But the mere observation of chromosomal differences between species does not support such a theory. Chromosomes vary within a species too, and it is just as possible that speciation takes place for some other reason, and chromosomal changes accumulate independently of speciation.

The observations, then, do not strongly support the theory of speciation by chromosomal change; but one interesting theoretical idea does. To understand it, we must return to the fundamental condition for the evolution of a new species. New species are likely to evolve whenever natural selection works against hybrid and heterozygous forms. In the simplest case, of one gene with two alleles (and three genotypes, AA, Aa, and aa), heterozygous disadvantage means that Aa individuals are inferior to AA and aa individuals. How will natural selection work in this case? The AA

homozygotes will be selected to mate with other AA homozygotes rather than with either of the other two genotypes, for if an AA mates an Aa or an aa, the disadvantaged Aa heterozygotes will be among the offspring. The aa homozygotes will likewise be selected to mate among themselves. The result will be two species, one for each homozygote. The disadvantageous matings will then not take place.

That is the general theory. Let us now see why it might particularly apply to chromosomal changes. We are looking for a reason why chromosomal changes might be disadvantageous in heterozygous form. One kind of chromosomal change is called an inversion. In an inversion, a section of the chromosome is reversed: if the original chromosome had eight genes in the order ABCDEFGH, then ABGFEDCH would be an inversion. Let us call the chromosomes with the original order C_1 and the inverted chromosomes C_2. (A letter now stands for a whole chromosome, rather than a single gene as it has done before.) Now, provided that it did not matter what order the chromosomes were in (which it often may do), the original and inverted form would be equivalent. The two homozygotes C_1C_1 and C_2C_2 would be indistinguishable and would give rise to equally good offspring. But now consider the heterozygote C_1C_2, which has one original and one inverted chromosome. The heterozygote itself would be just like either homozygote. The difficulty comes with reproduction (Figure 8). At reproduction, the genes on the pair of chromosomes are recombined. Recombination may take place at any point on the chromosomes, and there is a chance that it will occur somewhere in the inverted region; in which case the resultant chromosomes would lack some genes and have others in double copy. The offspring that lacked a full set of genes would probably be inviable.

Therefore, whenever there is a chromosomal inversion in a population, there will be selection for speciation. But the whole process from the appearance of a chromosomal inversion as a new mutation to the completion of speciation requires special conditions. In normal circumstances, the inversion C_2 will be selected against and eliminated as soon as it arises. When it first arises it will be a single copy in a heterozygote, C_1C_2. C_2 cannot

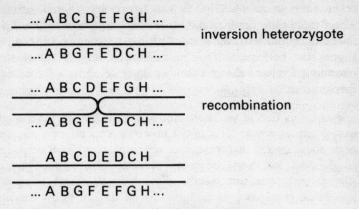

Fig. 8. Selection against inversion-heterozygotes.

The heterozygous organism bearing a chromosomal inversion possesses a full set of genes (symbolized A, B, C, etc.). But after recombination, the offspring chromosomes may lack some genes. The offspring that inherit such chromosomes would probably be at a disadvantage.

gradually increase in frequency until some C_2C_2 homozygotes are formed. If speciation is to take place at all, it will have to be quickly, soon after the mutant appears and before it is eliminated by selection against heterozygotes. This may be possible in one situation: inbreeding. If the offspring of the mutant C_1C_2 individuals mate together, they will probably produce, by Mendelian segregation, C_2C_2 homozygotes among their offspring. Once the C_2C_2 homozygotes have appeared, they will be selected to mate only with other C_2C_2 individuals rather than C_1C_2 or C_1C_1 individuals. C_1C_1 and C_2C_2 may split into two new species.

For a species to evolve from a mutant chromosomal inversion, inbreeding is essential. If the offspring of the mutant do not inbreed, they will mate with ordinary C_1C_1 individuals. No C_2C_2 mutant homozygotes will be produced by those matings, and the C_2 inversion will probably be eliminated before any C_2C_2 homozygotes arise.

The association of inbreeding and chromosomal speciation led Bush, Case, Wilson, and Patton to the following prediction. Kinds of animals that live in small groups, which are probably inbred, should have higher rates of chromosomal evolution than other kinds of animals that live in larger, less inbred, groups. They tested their prediction with 225 genera of vertebrates. They found the predicted association. It is not a strong proof; but it is suggestive. Perhaps there is something in all that speculative reasoning. Perhaps chromosomal changes do, at least sometimes, drive speciation.

Speciation is rich in problems but poor in solutions. This might have been expected. Most of the problems concern precise questions about events that took place in the past and have been, to a large extent, lost down the stream of history. But let me finish by summarizing our uncertainty. Both allopatric and sympatric speciation take place in nature, but we do not know for sure which is commoner. Nor do we know whether speciating populations are usually large or small. We can draw no positive conclusion on the extent of genetic changes at speciation, except to say that it is probably variable. On the nature of the genetic changes at speciation, we can conclude that only changes in mating habits are essential, and those trivially so, for they are required by definition. It is rather doubtful whether any other kinds of genetic changes are particularly associated with speciation, although some kinds of chromosomal change may be. Finally, the random loss of genes in small populations is of little or no importance in speciation: speciation, like most evolutionary processes, is probably powered by natural selection.

9 The Rates of Evolution

The rate of evolution is easily defined. It is simply the amount of change in a trait divided by the time the change took. It is not so easily measured in practice. The evidence must come from the fossil record, whose several incompletenesses supply a constant source of difficulties. Only traits preserved in fossils can be used. So, to measure the rate of evolution, one must start by picking an appropriate property of an abundantly preserved trait, such as teeth height in vertebrates. It is then measured in as many specimens as possible, drawn from different times. The specimens should be members of a single evolutionary lineage, because if the later forms are not the descendants of earlier forms the 'rate' of change between them is nonsense. But, assuming that an evolutionary lineage can be recognized, the rate of evolution is just the difference in the average state of the trait at two different times, divided by the amount of time separating them. Rates such as these have been measured for many traits in many different lineages. The evolutionary problem is to understand the patterns in the rates, why some lineages evolve faster than others, some traits faster than others, why individual lineages evolve at different rates at different times.

Rates of evolution could also be used to test the theory of evolution by natural selection. Natural selection takes time. For a mutant to increase in frequency from its initial rare state to become the normal gene in the whole population may take a few thousand generations. The exact amount of time can be calculated from equations first derived by J. B. S. Haldane in 1924; it depends on the gene's initial frequency and its selective advantage. A mutant that produces on average 1 per cent more offspring than its alternative allele, for instance, would take 4,266 generations to increase in frequency from 0.1 per cent to 99.9 per cent of the population. If the selective advantage of a particular change in a particular trait were known, Haldane's equation would predict how fast it should evolve under natural selection. The prediction could in principle be tested. In practice, no strong test of this kind has ever been possible. The evidence is not good enough. Our knowledge of genetics and selective advantages is too weak, let alone the quality of fossil evidence. The selective advantages of most evolutionary changes are probably not much more than a few per cent (and probably much less). We can predict that evolution should never go faster than such a selective advantage would allow. In fact the rates of evolution observed in the fossil record are well below that limit. This provides a test of Darwinism, for evolution could possibly go faster than Darwinism allows, and if it did we should need another theory: the fact that the rates are not too fast is evidence for the Darwinian theory. But the test is imprecise; the range of facts allowed by the theory is very wide.

The main interest of evolutionary rates lies elsewhere. It is in their variation between different periods and different groups. We should first consider whether the variation is real. The interpretation of evolutionary rates is confounded with problems of perception. Vertebrates for instance appear to evolve faster than invertebrates; mammals in particular have been said to evolve at about twice the rate of bivalve molluscs. This might be a genuine fact of evolution. It might then (perhaps) be explained by more intense competition and a more changeable force of selection among mammals than among molluscs. But, on the other hand, the difference in rate might be apparent rather than real. We are mammals ourselves, and more sensitive (it may be) to differences among creatures more similar to us: perhaps we simply cannot see differences between bivalve molluscs that are objectively as great as those we do notice between mammals. This would be a difficult hypothesis to test with fossil evidence. (It might more easily be tested with molecular evidence, which as we have seen (p. 63) is less subject to the biases of human observation.)

Philip Gingerich has discovered another perceptual problem in the study of evolutionary rates. Different estimates of evolutionary rates are usually measured over different time-intervals. The effect of time-interval (it has always been supposed) is removed by dividing by time in calculating the rate of evolution. But when Gingerich plotted many different estimates of rates of evolution against the time-interval of the estimate, he found a clear and negative relationship: as the time-interval decreased, the estimated rate of evolution increased. Gingerich's interpretation of his result is highly subversive. He noticed that the total amount of evolution was in all cases about the same: the differences in rate are entirely due to differences in the time-span of the samples. He suggests that we only pick on a certain degree of difference to measure. If two samples are very similar—if there has been almost no evolutionary change between them—it does not seem interesting to measure them; if two samples are very different, they do not look like the same thing, and it is difficult to measure them both in a comparable way: in either case the rate of evolution would not be measured. We are left with the in-between amounts of evolution, and it is these that have been measured. If Gingerich's argument is correct, the available measurements of evolutionary rates are a highly biased sample, and many comparisons of them may be artefactual.

Comparisons of evolutionary rates stand the best chance of being realistic if they concern the same lineage at different times, rather than different lineages. From now on, we shall be concerned with rates of evolution in single lineages. Our questions now are: Do lineages evolve at different rates at different times? If they do, why do they? These questions, although they have been asked for a century, have become of particular interest recently in a controversy concerning the hypothesis of punctuated equilibrium. The term was first used by Niles Eldredge and Stephen Gould in 1972. The theory of punctuated equilibrium suggests that evolution has an inconstant tempo, with short intervals of rapid evolution ('punctuations') interrupting much longer periods in which there is no evolutionary change. It also suggests that the intervals of rapid evolution are the occasion of speciation. Nearly all evolutionary change (the theory says) is concentrated in short intervals of speciation, at other times evolution stands still. Eldredge and Gould believe that punctuated equilibrium is the normal pattern of evolutionary rates; they contrast it with what they call phyletic gradualism. According to the theory of phyletic gradualism, the rate of evolution is constant; the rate of change is similar when a lineage is splitting and when it is not. In its extreme form, it would say that in all cases the rate of evolution is constant. No one holds that extreme theory; but extremes can still be of conceptual interest even when no one can be found to support them. We can identify the extremes, and try to test them. But a theory that claims to describe all evolution makes too combustible a straw man. Let us limit them a little. Let them lay claim to only a majority of cases. Majority, of course, is a vague word, but Gould's 'off-the-cuff claim for 90 per cent' gives it sufficient meaning: we can judge the theory of punctuated equilibrium to be correct if more than about 90 per cent of cases conform to it.

Which theory do the facts support? It has been known for over a century that fossil lineages generally appear suddenly in the fossil record, persist for a few million years, and then disappear abruptly without merging into any later lineages. At least since Darwin this pattern has been attributed to the incompleteness of the fossil record, not to the process of evolution. No one, then or now, doubts that there are gaps in the fossil record. It is riddled with them. No one doubts what the effect of the gaps is. They make evolution appear less gradual than it actually was. Gaps in the fossil record appear as jumps in evolution. Therefore, if we wish to use the fossil record to test between the two theories, we should first find out whether it is good enough. It must be complete enough for the record of a punctuated pattern of evolution to differ from that of gradual evolution. Let us consider how complete the fossil record is.

The reasons for the incompleteness of the fossil record are well known. For a fossil to be left, it must be preserved and in a place where sediments are being deposited. Both processes may fail. Indeed, the preservation of an animal in recognizable form is a highly unlikely event. It must be transported to, or die in, the kind of environment in which sediments are laid down; the sediments must be laid down quickly enough for the dead animal not to be destroyed in the meantime by decomposition, but the environment must be gentle enough for the animal not to be smashed beyond all subsequent recognition. With that set of necessary conditions we need not be surprised that so few animals are preserved as fossils even where sediments are laid down. But what of the process of sedimentation itself? Obvious gaps in the sedimentary record can be detected by changes in chemistry and appearance. But let us concentrate on the regions, that are more likely to be continuous, between the obvious gaps. How complete are they? Several geologists have recently tried to answer this question, using the following method. They first measure the short-term rate of deposition of sediments, over some humanly manageable interval such as 10–100 years, in places such as rivers, lakes, and estuaries. They then measure the thickness (with a ruler) and the total duration (by standard radiometry) of a sedimentary unit in the fossil record. Its 'completeness' can be estimated as

$$\frac{\text{total thickness}}{\text{total time} \times \text{short-term rate of deposition}}$$

If the short-term rate of deposition had been kept up throughout the period, the fraction would be one; and the record would be 'complete'. Schindel has recently calculated the completeness of several of the best fossil sequences that have been discussed in the debate over punctuated equilibria. I have simplified his results in Table 2. The important point to notice in the Table is that the numbers are all much less than one. I should emphasize that these figures are for some of the best records we have. Typical figures might be more like 0.1, 0.01, or less. That means that for every hundred years of real time, sediments were only laid down for ten years, one year, or less. And, as we have seen, even while sediments are being deposited, fossils may not be deposited as well.

The fossil record therefore is demonstrably incomplete. For this reason, I do not think that a century of palaeontological experience of the general pattern of the fossil record can be used to test whether or not evolution is gradual. Some supporters of the theory of punctuated equilibrium have cited in their own favour the common observation of the sudden appearance and disappearance of species in the fossil record. But this observation is common ground between the two theories. It cannot decide

Table 2 Completeness of some sedimentary records

Subject	Authority	Completeness
Eocene mammals	Gingerich	0.28
Permian foraminiferids	Ozawa	0.04
Neogene radiolaria	Kellogg	0.02
Neogene foraminiferids	Malmgren and Kennett	0.23
Jurassic ammonites	Raup and Crick	0.03
Pennsylvanian snails	Schindel	0.34
Plio-pleistocene molluscs	Williamson 1	0.45
	2	0.73

Simplified from Schindel.

between them. One theory attributes it to gaps in the record, the other to the mode of evolution. Neither theory predicts that new species should not appear suddenly in the fossil record.

The few cases in which the record is known to be relatively complete might be more decisive. Even in these the record is far from fully complete. The best have completenesses of only about one half. But they are the best evidence we have. The punctuationist would predict that the pattern of change should look similar in more and in less complete records; the gradualist that more complete records should reveal one lineage smoothly evolving into another.

Unfortunately only a few lineages with a relatively complete fossil record have been thoroughly studied. There are not enough to be conclusive. But it is worth mentioning two cases, one of probable punctuated evolution and the other of probable gradual evolution, if only to show that both modes of evolution do take place.

For an example of punctuated evolution we can return to Williamson's snails, which we met in the last chapter. As we saw then, his interpretation of the changes in the snails through time is controversial; some experts think that they may not be evolutionary genetic changes at all, but phenotypic switches caused by changes in the environment. Again, we shall here tentatively follow Williamson's interpretation. The fossil snails are spread through many metres of sediments east of Lake Turkana in Kenya. The record has been analysed by Schindel and, as the Table shows, two different parts of Williamson's study have completenesses of 0.45 and 0.73, which are high enough for his results to be of interest to us. The snails show a punctuated equilibrial pattern of evolution: there are long periods during which the snails do not change, and short intervals of sudden change. After a change, the new forms are sufficiently different to count as new species; punctuation and speciation therefore coincide. The snails of Lake Turkana fit the pattern of punctuated equilibrium. We shall return to the explanation later.

For an example of gradual evolution, we can turn from snails to mammals. Gingerich has documented gradual evolution in several species of North American mammals. The sedimentary completeness of his site is 0.28, as the Table shows. His best-known case is from an extinct group of mammals called condylarths, particularly the genus *Hyopsodus*. Like Williamson's, but for different reasons, Gingerich's study is controversial. We shall tentatively follow Gingerich's interpretation here. His measurements are all of tooth size. In the period studied, *Hyopsodus* split three or four times. The rate of evolution at splitting appears to be approximately the same as the rate of change within a species when it is not splitting. Change within a species and speciation were both gradual; Gingerich's condylarths fit the theory of gradual evolution.

Evolution therefore can be gradual or jerky. So far, at all events, we do not have enough facts to say whether one mode is more frequent; but this shortage of facts has not prevented the development of theories. Several reasons have been suggested to explain (what is not confirmed) why the rate of evolution is highly inconstant, and why nearly all evolutionary change is concentrated in rapid bouts of speciation. Although these theories are speculative and may have no application in the real world, they do still merit some discussion. Let us discuss them.

The explanation of gradual evolution is less controversial. Provided that the rate of evolution is not so constant as to suggest a random walk (see p. 66), the most plausible explanation is that evolution is being driven by a fairly constant force of natural selection. This is not the only explanation. A constant trend would also appear through time if specimens from two different samples were mixed together, with the exact mixture progressively changing. The first sample might contain only one species, *A*; the second, a few specimens of another species, *B*, mixed in but unrecognized, with a majority of specimens of species *A*; and then later and later samples containing relatively more and more of species *B*. The average of each sample would gradually move from that of pure *A* to pure *B*. This kind of artefact can be tested for, and is probably not often important. Natural selection is the most likely explanation of gradual evolutionary trends.

If there is only one uncontroversial explanation of gradual evolution, there are several highly controversial candidate explanations of punctuated equilibria. Each must be able to explain both periods without change and occasional punctuations, as well as why the punctuations should coincide with speciation.

There are two possible explanations of the periods without evolutionary change: natural selection and constraint. We have dealt with them as general alternatives before, in Chapter 4. The theory of natural selection would explain the absence of evolutionary change by stabilizing (also called normalizing) selection. Stabilizing selection means that natural selection favours the average type. It is probably the usual mode of natural selection. It has been demonstrated in several cases. The best known is human birth-weight. Within a human population, babies born with average weight have a higher chance of survival than heavier or lighter babies. Natural selection is holding the birth-weight constant; it is stabilizing. By contrast, the theory of constraint denies that natural selection has anything to do with evolutionary stability. Species remain unchanged (it says) because they are incapable of changing, because the necessary heritable variants cannot arise. Just why they cannot arise is another question, to which several answers have been suggested: that the mutations would be incompatible with the way the organism develops ('developmental constraint'), or genetically impossible ('genetical constraint'), and so on: all such suggestions are speculative—there is no evidence for them—but, in some cases, plausible.

We typically lack the evidence to decide whether evolutionary stability, in any particular case, is caused by stabilizing selection or constraint. But (as we have seen, p. 57) the theory of constraint can be tested. If the trait shows heritable variation, it cannot be constrained; if it does not, it may be. Human birth-weight, for instance, is probably not held constant by a constraint, because it is known to vary within human populations. The same line of reasoning can, more tentatively, be used for fossils. If a modern form is known which resembles the fossil, we can extrapolate from the one to the other. We have seen that Williamson's snails remained constant for long periods. Was that (we can ask) because of stabilizing selection or a constraint? The shells of modern snails, similar to the fossils of Lake Turkana, do vary and the variation is heritable. If (as is likely) the fossil snails shared this property with modern ones, their evolutionary constancy was not due to a constraint on variation.

The intervals of rapid change also need to be explained, and why they are connected with speciation. Eldredge and Gould originally explained both by the process of speciation. We saw, in the last chapter, that the exact nature of the process of speciation is not known; but it may often be accomplished by the geographical splitting of a single ancestral species. Consider how allopatric speciation would be recorded in the sediments at any one place. Initially there would be the ancestral species. As it split, the speciating population would not be recorded, because it would be situated elsewhere. The descendent species would only appear in the record if it re-invaded the range of its ancestor. When it did, it would be a fully formed new species, and would appear in the record suddenly. If it drove its ancestor extinct, there would be a sudden replacement. Thus allopatric speciation would be recorded in fossils as a pattern of punctuated equilibrium. This would be so whatever the actual rate of evolution during speciation. The mere pattern of rapid evolution at speciation, in the fossil record, may not mean that evolution is especially rapid then. It may only mean that speciation is allopatric.

There are further possibilities. We have considered whether speciating populations are small. The evidence does not suggest that they are, but the evidence is slight and may be wrong. If speciating populations were small, they would be less likely to leave a fossil record, and the evolution of a new species would have less chance of being recorded.

Another effect of small population size has been suggested, although it is far less certain. Evolution may proceed more quickly in smaller populations. If it did, small populations would have less chance of leaving records as fossils. When evolution is rapid, each particular stage lasts for a shorter time. But is evolution faster in smaller populations? One simple model predicts the exact opposite. If the rate of evolution depends on the rate at which mutational improvements arise, evolution will be faster in larger populations because the total number of mutations per generation is higher in a larger population than a smaller one. We have already met a more complex model (p. 119), in which evolution proceeds faster in *subdivided* populations. That is when natural selection opposes mutations in the heterozygote but favours them as homozygotes. But the effect here is due to the subdivision, not the total size, of the population. There is in theory no reason to suppose that evolution is faster in smaller populations. If speciating populations are smaller than other populations, only the effect of size on the chance of leaving a fossil record can be used in the explanation of sudden changes in the fossil record.

The facts however do not need to be explained by any special process of speciation. The only fact that may need explanation is that evolution may proceed faster at some times than at others. Natural selection alone can explain that. Because punctuated evolution has sometimes been said to contradict natural selection, I should emphasize that natural selection has no difficulty in explaining the rates of evolution found in geological punctuations. On a human time-scale, natural selection is a slow process. With organisms, such as bacteria or even fruitflies, which have short generation times, it is possible to produce noticeable evolutionary change in a few days or weeks. But outside the laboratory we do not normally notice evolutionary change. It has taken thousands of years to produce the present diversity of kinds of dogs, even though the changes were probably relatively rapid. Natural evolution is scarcely observable at all. Human experience however is no guide to the geological scale of time. A change that is too slow for us to notice can pass in a geological instant. The evolution of Williamson's snails was concentrated in a tiny part of the sedimentary column, but it in fact corresponds to a time of between 5,000 and 50,000 years. In that amount of time, natural selection could produce a large change, much greater than what actually took place. Moreover, the bouts of rapid evolution coincided with changes in sea level, which would be times of rapid environmental change. When the environment changes, natural selection will probably favour a new form. If Williamson's snails did evolve, their evolution was probably driven by natural selection. The facts alone at least do not rule out conventional natural selection. No special evolutionary process, or particular theory of speciation, is required. As we go on (as we now shall) to consider some more heterodox ideas, we must bear in mind that it is not the facts that demand them.

The heterodox explanation of punctuations is macro-mutation. A macro-mutation is a mutation large enough to produce a form outside the normal range of variation of a species. By definition, they must be rare, or they would fall within the normal range of a species variation. The explanation of punctuated evolution by macro-mutation is straightforward. The macro-mutations are the punctuations. When one of these macro-mutations crops up, if it survives, it will produce a large and rapid evolutionary change; because they are rare, there will be long periods of stability between each macro-mutation. If a theory is heterodox it will have its supporters, but it is just worth summarizing why most evolutionary biologists doubt the importance of macro-mutations. For a start, there is little evidence that they ever occur; evolution based on small variations, by contrast, is a well-studied and well-understood process. Moreover, no known facts require explanation by macro-mutation. And then it is difficult to understand how a macro-mutation could ever be advantageous. An organism is a finely tuned machine. Small adjustments may, by a rare chance, be improvements; but large changes are much less likely to be. This places a strict limit on the kinds of evolutionary events that macro-mutations even in principle can account for. The evolution of new complex adaptations must have required many stages; their evolution by macro-mutation is theoretically so unlikely as to be impossible (p. 41). Macro-mutations can in principle explain rapid evolution if it is not adaptive, but not the rapid evolution of novel and complex adaptations.

A final objection applies more generally. Any theory which insists that evolution can only proceed in the pattern of punctuated equilibrium, and which explains that pattern by some special but necessary process, will run into difficulty with the facts of intra-specific variation. One kind of intra-specific variation is geographic variation. It is often gradual, and can be of sufficient extent to produce speciation, as we have seen in the ring species of gulls (p. 6). Geographic variation is also, to some extent, genetic. If evolution can be gradual, genetic, and large enough to produce speciation in space, then it can too in time, for there is no fundamental difference between evolution in time and space. Any theory which declares that speciation cannot take place in small stages should be disconcerted by ring species.

A more flexible theory of macro-mutation might admit that macro-mutations are not a necessary hypothesis. It might merely plead that they are possible. The most hopeful place to look for macro-mutations is in the genetics of development and regulation. Genetical changes affecting early events in development may be more likely to have large effects in the adult than later-acting ones. Similarly, changes in regulatory genes (genes that control the expression of other genes) may produce bigger effects than changes in non-regulatory genes. Of the known genetical differences between species, the ones that (it has been suggested) are most likely to be regulatory are those in the chromosomes. It is possible that regulatory genes lie next door on the chromosomes to the genes they regulate. An inversion (p. 118) therefore might remove a regulated gene from its regulator, which might result in a very large change.

We can carry this speculation one stage further. Chromosomal changes, as we have seen, may be particularly likely to produce speciation, and they may cause particularly rapid speciation. Perhaps all these properties are connected. Perhaps a grand genetical theory of punctuated equilibria will be formulated out of them. All that need be said for now, however, is that we do not have any reason to suppose that one will.

The problem of whether the rate of evolution is fairly constant or highly variable has not been solved. Its solution is a matter of fact. But the facts must come from exceptionally complete fossil records, and too few of them have been studied to allow a conclusion to be drawn. When one is, there will be many theories waiting to explain it. But the various theories of punctuated equilibrium cannot be tested by fossil evidence: they could only be tested by the study of speciation in living forms.

10 Macro-evolution

Most of the evidence of large-scale evolutionary change (which is conveniently called macro-evolution) comes from the fossil record. Only in the fossil record can we watch evolution for long enough to be able to detect large-scale patterns. It reveals, for instance, the rise and fall of groups at all taxonomic levels: species and genera come and go, and so too do the families, orders, and classes that contain them. The larger more inclusive groups do of course last longer, but the pattern for all groups is the same. Then there are mass extinctions, in which several large groups go extinct at about the same time. We can also see, within lineages, evolutionary trends, in which the members of the lineage evolve continually in the same direction, through many species and over a long period of time. Such are the phenomena of macro-evolution.

The explanation of macro-evolution presents a set of individual problems, of the form 'why did group A take over from group B through time T?', or 'why did group C go extinct at time S?' But here we shall not be concerned with problems of individual groups. We shall be concerned with the more general question of whether the facts of macro-evolution can be explained by the theories that we have used for smaller changes, or whether they must be explained by higher-level theories which, conceptually, only apply to macro-evolution. Is macro-evolution merely micro-evolution summed up over long periods of time, or is it controlled by different processes?

Let us consider evolutionary trends first. What, exactly, is an evolutionary trend? The tendency for animals to become bigger as a lineage evolves provides an example; it is well enough known to have been given a name, Cope's rule. The nineteenth-century American palaeontologist Edward Drinker Cope never explicitly formulated the rule, but he did demonstrate the fact, for mammals at least, which is why it is named after him. Instances of Cope's rule can be found in all the mammalian groups, with the possible exception of bats. The ancestors of modern marsupials were no bigger than modern rats; modern wolves are larger than ancestral canids; the Eocene ancestors of the modern camels and llamas were about the size of a hare; and the Eocene *Moeritherium*, which was probably related to the ancestors of the modern elephant, was about the size of a tapir. Cases of size decrease are known in the evolution of mammals; but they are the exception, not the rule.

It might be argued that Cope's rule is a mammalian peculiarity. Perhaps the ancestors of many modern mammalian groups were small in order to avoid competition with larger reptiles, and have only increased in size to occupy, after the extinction of the dinosaurs, the formerly reptilian niches. That may be the explanation of Cope's rule in mammals; but the rule is more general. Cases of evolutionary size increase have been found in every major group of animals that is represented in the fossil record. The rule can be found at work among cephalopods, snails, echinoderms, and those single-celled organisms called foraminiferids which leave such abundant fossil remains.

Cope's 'rule' may not in fact be a real rule. Its supporters may have selected the cases that conform to it from a mass of cases that point in all directions. It has been estimated that the rule only applies to about two-thirds of all cases, which might make a sceptic doubt whether it really is a genuine rule. The true degree of generality is a question of fact which it would be out of place to settle here. I only intend to use Cope's rule as an example of the kind of thing which we are trying to explain. It is (if valid) a macro-evolutionary trend. Other trends are known from the fossil record. Dollo's law, that the direction of evolution does not reverse, is one. Another is Williston's law, that evolution in segmented organisms proceeds from a state in which all the segments are much the same towards a state in which the segments are more and more differentiated. Like Cope's rule, these other rules have exceptions. But we only need one example to support a theoretical discussion, and even a hypothetical example would do. Cope's rule is probably not entirely hypothetical: there is probably some truth in it: let us, for sake of argument, suppose that it contains truth enough to merit some attempt at explanation.

There are two main kinds of explanation. According to the first, the continual increase in size, through one species after another of the lineage, is powered by a continual force of natural selection in favour of larger size. Just why natural selection should favour larger size is another problem. Rensch has listed several possibilities: larger animals are more likely than their smaller conspecifics to win fights, especially as they will probably have larger weapons; they may have larger brains, which may make them more intelligent; they may live longer. All, none, or just some, of these theories may be correct; there are other possibilities as well, but we do not need to examine them here. All that matters is that if natural selection favours larger size, year in year out for millions of years, there will probably be a trend towards larger size. If a trend has been directed by natural selection it will look like the ones illustrated in the centre column of Figure 9.

The second explanation supposes that natural selection does not favour larger size. The trend is explained instead by the effects of the trait (body size in this case) on the rate of speciation and the longevity of the species. This has come to be called the theory of species selection. It can work on both speciation rate and species longevity, which we shall take in turn.

Suppose that those species made up of larger organisms split into new species at a higher rate than do species made up of smaller organisms. The speciation rate (it is supposed) is not higher because natural selection, within each species, favours larger body size: there could be stabilizing selection for size within the species, or size might not be affected by natural selection at all. The difference in speciation rates would have to be for some other reason. Perhaps, for instance, the larger-sized members of the large-bodied species do not move as far as the smaller members of the smaller-bodied species; with less movement, gene flow around the species' range would be reduced; the species would be more likely to be split into several geographically isolated populations; and they, in turn, might evolve into new species.

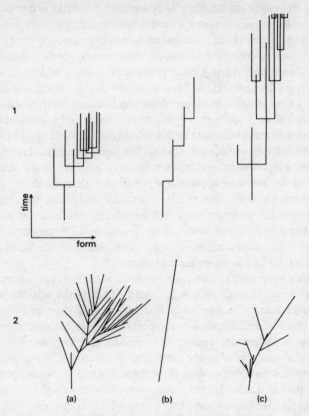

Fig. 9. Species selection and natural selection of evolutionary trends.

In all six cases there is a trend towards larger body size. Speciation occurs when a lineage splits: (1) in the three cases at the top the rate of evolution is faster when a lineage splits than within a lineage between splits; (2) in the three cases at the bottom the rate of evolution is much the same at a split and between splits. The two cases are included to illustrate that the following distinction is independent of the rate of evolution at times of splitting. In the centre column (b) the trend is driven by natural selection: the direction of speciation is usually the same as the direction of the total trend. In columns (a) and (c) the trend is driven by two kinds of species selection: in both, speciation is as likely to be in the opposite direction to the total trend (i.e. to the left on the page) as in the same direction. (a) species selection by differential rates of speciation: the rate of splitting increases as the species' body size increases. (c) species selection by differential species longevity: the longevity of species increases as the species' body size increases.

But the exact explanation does not matter. What is necessary is that for some reason species with a higher average body size split at a higher rate than species with a lower average body size. Species selection will then produce a trend towards species with larger body size. In the pure process of species selection, speciation itself is undirected. New species, as they arise, are just as likely to be smaller as larger than their ancestor: they must be, because the only force that could direct speciation is natural selection, and natural selection *ex hypothesi* is not operating. The trend is produced by selection among the new species. Those new species whose members happen to have a larger body size will produce further new species at a higher rate than do those species whose members happen to have a smaller body size. Species with larger and larger body sizes will proliferate therefore at an ever increasing rate, until some limit is reached. A trend towards species with larger members will take place, of the kind illustrated in the left-hand column of Figure 9.

A similar process, also called species selection, can operate on species longevity. Cope's rule would result if the species whose members have a larger body size last longer over evolutionary time. As before, the theory supposes that natural selection does not favour larger size within each species, and that new species of smaller animals arise at the same rate as species of larger animals. Species that last longer will, if speciation rate is constant, produce more descendants. In this case, we are supposing that larger-bodied species last longer than smaller-bodied species. They will produce more descendent species and, therefore, proliferate. The trend characteristic of Cope's rule will be produced. Figure 9 illustrates it at the right.

Species selection is like natural selection, but at a different level. Natural selection works by the differential survival and fecundity of individual organisms; species selection on the differential survival and fecundity of species. The variation affected by natural selection is produced by genetic mutation; the variation affected by species selection by speciation. Just as mutation is random in the sense that its direction is unrelated to what natural selection favours, so, under species selection, the direction of speciation is unrelated to the direction of the evolutionary trend.

Just as natural selection only works on heritable variation, so, if species selection is to operate, new species must be relatively like their parental species. For instance, in the case of Cope's rule, although larger-bodied species produce both large and smaller-bodied descendants, the descendants of larger-bodied species must (on average) be larger than the descendants of a smaller-bodied species. If the heritable variation of any trait is correlated with individual survival and fecundity, natural selection will inevitably work on it; if the variation of any trait is correlated with species longevity and speciation rate, species selection will inevitably work on it.

Natural and species selection could, in theory, conflict. Species selection might oppose a trait that natural selection favoured. In such a case, natural selection would win: the trait favoured by natural selection but opposed by species selection would predominate in the species. The reason is the same as we met when discussing group selection in Chapter 4, that natural selection is much faster than species selection. The units on which species selection must work only arise rarely: they are new species, which arise perhaps at the rate of once every few thousand generations. The units on which natural selection works are individual organisms, which arise in great numbers every generation. Natural selection must be several million times faster than species selection: any race between them will be easily won by natural selection.

Because species selection is so slow a process, it can also be ruled out as an explanation of the evolution of complex adaptations. The evolution of adaptations requires the selection of many small changes (p. 41), which could never be assembled by the slow process of species selection. Even if ordinary natural selection is displaced by species selection from the explanation of some evolutionary trends, it remains the only explanation of the evolution of adaptation. Adaptive trends must be driven by natural selection; pure species selection can apply at most only to simple trends: it might drive a change in body size; but not the evolution of an eye.

If natural selection is not favouring any directional change, in parallel, within each species, species selection will be left free to work. The two processes could also reinforce each other. For this reason, although the two processes differ they are not strictly alternatives. One could ask, of any particular trend, how much it owed to natural, and how much to species, selection.

The theory of species selection has not yet been applied to a real evolutionary trend; but it is testable. A trend driven by species selection should leave two tell-tale features in a complete fossil record. One is the direction of change when each new species arises, which should be unrelated to the direction of the total trend in the lineage of many species. In the case of a trend to increased body size, new smaller-bodied species should appear at the same rate as new larger-bodied species. If the trend was being produced by natural selection, however, speciation would be in the direction of the trend. The prediction of species selection, therefore, is strong: it is clearly different from that of natural selection. The second feature is that larger-bodied species should last longer or speciate at a higher rate. This could also be tested, but it is not such a strong prediction. If the trend were being driven by natural selection, the same observation might be expected: if natural selection favoured larger body size, larger individuals would probably live longer, and one might well expect a species made up of larger individuals to last longer in evolutionary time. Facts bearing on either prediction, and especially on the first, would be of great interest. Unfortunately, none exist.

Species selection was first suggested, as an explanation of evolutionary trends by Eldredge and Gould, in the same paper in which they put forward their hypothesis of punctuated equilibrium (which we discussed in the last chapter). They did not actually coin the term species selection, which is due to S. M. Stanley. According to Eldredge and Gould, their two hypotheses are related. They treat species selection as a consequence of punctuated equilibrium. Many evolutionary biologists have followed them, but, I believe, they are in error. Whether speciation is sudden or gradual makes no difference to whether evolutionary trends are driven by species selection.

We have discussed the requirements for species selection, and to repeat them will be enough to prove that they are completely independent of the relative rate of evolution at speciation. For species selection to produce a trend, the direction of speciation should be unrelated to the direction of the trend, the state of the trait (undergoing the trend) should be correlated with the rate of speciation or species longevity, and the trend should not be opposed by natural selection. If those three requirements are met, species selection will take place. None of them have anything to do with the rate of evolution during speciation. The hypotheses of species selection and of punctuated equilibrium are completely independent of each other. I have emphasized this in Figure 9 by drawing the three kinds of evolutionary trend with both gradual and punctuated evolution at speciation.

So much for evolutionary trends. Let us now turn to evolution on an even grander scale. Let us consider the rise and fall of whole groups of species. If we examine the fossil record of a group, such as the cartilaginous fishes (now represented by sharks and rays), we see the number of species in it slowly increase up to a maximum and then decline. The same pattern can be seen at all levels: it is as true of a family of fish as it is of a whole sub-class of them. The only groups that do not both rise and fall in the fossil record are those, such as mammals, that have yet to go into a decline. The number of species of mammals has been increasing for about 60 million years, and shows no sign of having reached its maximum, let alone its decline. But within the group of mammals, some smaller groups, such as the Notoungulata (earlier relatives of modern ungulates), have completed their rise and final fall. Although the general pattern may be interrupted by temporary set-backs and secondary rounds of proliferation, it is clear enough to invite some attempt at explanation.

One is that a large group rises as it replaces another inferior group and then falls as it is in turn replaced by a superior group. The grand patterns of turnover in the fossil record are then due to competition between groups. Within this first hypothesis, there are two (alternative) sub-hypotheses to explain why one group should be competitively superior to another. We may call them progress and environmental change.

According to the theory of evolutionary progress, each succeeding group possesses some inherent advantage over the group that it replaces. The gait of early reptiles, for instance, is what is called (the term itself is judgemental) a sprawling gait, in which the legs stick out from the sides of the body and bend downwards to the ground, through 90°, at the knee-joint. Modern lizards and crocodiles retain the gait. The gait of mammals, by contrast, is an upright gait in which the legs point straight down from the body. For reasons which derive directly from the laws of mechanics, an animal with an upright gait can move faster (other things being equal) than an animal with a sprawling gait. It is tempting therefore to see the evolution of the upright gait as a progressive improvement. The eventual replacement of reptiles by mammals would then have resulted from this (and other) inherent superiorities of the mammalian body plan.

Modern evolutionary biologists, however, have become reluctant to explain evolutionary replacements by the hypothesis of evolutionary progress. One reason is that (as we saw in Chapter 4) we can expect animals to be adapted to their environments: there seems to be plenty of genetic variation for all traits, which should enable natural selection to effect all possible improvements. If an upright gait were good for crocodiles, we should expect them to evolve it. Another reason for the neglect of the hypothesis of progress is more practical. It is difficult to determine whether a change between groups really is an inherent improvement. The meaning of progress in theory is easy to define. One need only imagine, as a thought-experiment, putting the two groups into competition. We should put the mammals of today into competition with their reptilian equivalents of the Permian period 250 million years ago, in the environment of that time. If evolution was progressive, the modern mammal should eliminate its reptilian competitor. The competition should be as unequal as a battle between a modern destroyer and a sixteenth-century man-of-war. If, on the other hand, evolution was not progressive, the mammal would not win. But although the theoretical meaning of progress is clear, the practical experiment is impossible. Nor do we have a convincing method of simulating it. We are left with rather subjective judgements of which forms are progressive and which not. Scientists have little time for subjective judgements. Evolutionary progress therefore is now not much discussed.

The alternative to progress is that some kinds of organisms are better adapted than others to particular environments. Then, when the environment changes, the better-adapted form will replace the inferior. The difference from the hypothesis of progress is that here the advantages of one group over another are contingent rather than inherent. When one group has an advantage, it is only because the state of the environment happens, temporarily, to favour it: if the environment were changed, the advantage might be reversed. In terms of our earlier thought-experiment of competition between Permian reptiles and modern mammals, the outcome should depend on the environment of the encounter. In a Permian environment, the Permian reptile should win; in a modern environment, the modern mammal. This thought-experiment is equally difficult to perform; and accordingly we do not know whether the great evolutionary replacements were driven by environmental change. The hypothesis that different groups are adapted to different environments does however have a practical advantage over the hypothesis of progress: there are methods by which it can be tested (which we discussed in Chapter 4). Those methods however can only be applied with conviction to modern forms. It is, at present, difficult to apply them to the great evolutionary turnovers of the past, which accordingly remain unexplained. We do not know how much evolutionary turnover is caused by environmental change and how much by progressive improvement.

But these are not the only alternatives. The different groups may not be in competition. Their evolution (it is in principle possible) might be independent of one another, and their rise and fall a matter of luck. We shall explore two forms of this idea, taking first a modest form of it concerning replacements after mass extinctions, and then an ambitious theory of the entire pattern of evolution in the fossil record.

A mass extinction is an occasion in the fossil record when many different groups go extinct at the same time. Groups are always going extinct, but a number of times since the beginning of the fossil record the detectable rate of extinction has risen above the background level. Just what that number is is controversial; one estimate, by D. M. Raup and J. J. Sepkoski, makes it four (Figure 10). The best-known mass extinction is at the end of the

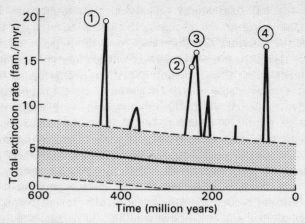

Fig. 10. Extinction rate (per million years) for families of marine animals through time up to the present.

Normal rates lie in the thick band; notice that the average rate declines with time. There are also four peaks, when mass extinctions took place; no. 4 was the occasion of the extinction of the dinosaurs at the end of the Cretaceous. (Simplified from Raup and Sepkoski.)

Cretaceous, 60 million years ago, when the dinosaurs suddenly disappeared.

There are many explanations of mass extinctions, but palaeontologists in general do not favour any particular theory. We are not going to consider the question here. We might, however, mention one of them to illustrate a theory of the turnover of groups. It has been suggested that mass extinctions are caused by disastrous rare physical events such as the collision of the earth with a large meteor. Some evidence favours the theory, other evidence does not: it is controversial. But let us admit it for the purpose of a different argument. A meteoric collision, together with its ensuing dust clouds and tidal waves, would be an indiscriminate killer. A few groups might survive it, but they might owe their survival more to luck than their adaptations. (They might not, but that is another matter.) If so, the replacements of one group by another would not be due to the competitive superiority of the successful group over the unsuccessful one. It might be due to the fortunes of survival in the disaster. Chance survival in a mass extinction is a possible explanation of replacements in the fossil record.

Here we have a hypothesis that can be tested. Let us consider it in a real example, the replacement of brachiopods by bivalves. Early in the fossil record, brachiopods were the more abundant group. They still survive, but they are now relatively rare compared with bivalve molluscs. Brachiopods and bivalves would probably compete with each other, if placed together, because they lead quite similar kinds of life. Now, why have bivalves replaced brachiopods? There are two hypotheses: that bivalves have driven brachiopods extinct by competitive superiority, and that bivalves were the fortunate survivors of a mass extinction in which brachiopods succumbed. The test is to examine the relative abundances of the groups before and after each mass extinction. (If the replacement took place between mass extinctions, then clearly one hypothesis is ruled out; but the replacement of brachiopods by molluscs took place around the Permo-Triassic mass extinction.)

What, exactly, should we look for? If the replacement is due to competitive superiority, the superior group should increase continually relative to the other. Even before the mass extinction, bivalves should be increasing relative to brachiopods. If the replacement was pure luck, the relative abundances should be roughly constant before the mass extinction; then one of the groups, the brachiopods in this case, should go extinct (or almost extinct) while the other survived, and proliferated afterwards.

The relevant analysis has been performed for brachiopods and bivalves by Stephen Gould and Bradford Calloway (Figure 11). Before the mass extinction at the end of the Permian, brachiopods were declining and bivalves increasing, which suggests that the replacement is at least in part due to the competitive superiority of the bivalves. Then, at the mass extinction, the brachiopods suffered more than the bivalves. This could be a further consequence of competition between the groups, with the intensity of competition being increased by whatever circumstances were causing the mass extinction. Alternatively, the lower rate of extinction of the bivalves at the mass extinction might have been mere luck, in which case the replacement would have been caused by a

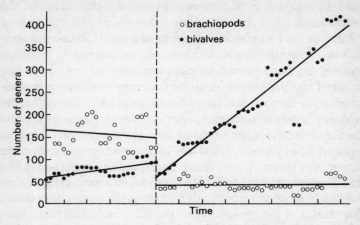

Fig. 11. Changes in the diversity of brachiopods and bivalves through time.

The vertical line marks the mass extinction at the end of the Permian. Before it brachiopods were more abundant, although slowly declining relative to bivalves; after the mass extinction bivalves were more abundant. At the mass extinction brachiopods declined much more than the bivalves. (From Gould and Calloway.)

combination of the competitive superiority of the bivalves before and after the mass extinction and their better fortune in it. In summary, Gould and Calloway's analysis cannot rule out a contribution from luck, and it provides positive evidence that the competitive superiority of the bivalves did contribute to the replacement.

So far we have only considered how luck might cause evolutionary replacements around mass extinctions. We must now consider the possibility that all the grand patterns of the fossil record are due to chance. We must first establish what chance means here. Imagine the following model of evolution. Each 'species' is represented by a set of states of a number of 'traits'. In a simple model there might be five traits, each with five possible states. The traits might represent such things as neck length and number of spines on back; their states would then be numbers, such as 1 inch, 1½ inch, etc. for neck length, and 4, 5, 6, etc. for spine number. The chance of evolutionary change can be represented in the model by a probability that any one state of a trait will change, in a generation, to another state. In the simplest model the probabilities for all the transitions would be the same. When this model is simulated in a computer, it shows 'evolution' in the sense that the species change through time.

Two other factors are needed to make the model more realistic. One is that each species should have a chance of splitting into two species, in order that new species can appear; the other is that each species should have a chance of survival from one generation to the next which is less than one, in order that species may sometimes go extinct. When these extra properties are added, the model shows an evolutionary pattern that closely resembles real evolution: groups arise, multiply, and go extinct; they occasionally evolve in recognizable evolutionary trends; they even show convergence, when different groups come to look like each other.

Although the behaviour of the model resembles evolution, the changes are not driven by natural selection. All changes are due to chance. Natural selection has not been built into the model: the evolution is all caused by the probabilistic transition of one state of a trait into another. The chance of any particular change, therefore, is independent of both the present states of a species and also of the states of all other species. There can be no competition, because one species does not affect another.

Such is the meaning of a random model of evolution. The important conclusion from these models, when they have been simulated, is that they show all the general patterns that can be seen in the fossil record. This does not mean, however, that evolution is only random change. But it does mean that we should not too facilely suggest particular explanations for particular instances of the rise, fall, and replacement of major groups. These phenomena would be expected sometimes even if evolution were random.

A strong test of the random theory of evolutionary patterns is not easy. We should need to know whether the evolutionary changes of random models have exactly the form and the frequency of real evolution in the fossil record. Some attempts at comparison have been made; but they have been inconclusive. The difficulty is that the class of random models that we have just discussed is large and versatile. By juggling with the exact values of the probabilities of speciation, extinction, and transitions between different states, it is possible to simulate almost any pattern of evolution. Random models are difficult to reject merely by the pattern of evolution in the fossil record, because some random model can be found to fit many different patterns.

The random model of evolution provides us with a third possible explanation of evolutionary trends. We have discussed two, natural selection and species selection; but we can now add the possibility that a short trend might just be the play of chance, the equivalent of tossing several heads in a row with a coin. But because a run of heads does not continue for long, chance cannot explain trends that continue over many generations in a consistent direction, or proceed in several independent evolutionary lineages. Chance could only produce short trends in single lineages. The random model remains as a caution against the conclusion that, whenever there is a trend, either species selection or natural selection must have been at work. In some cases, they may not.

This chapter has left us with two main unsolved problems of evolution. For those evolutionary trends that are not random, there are two main hypotheses. They may be powered by natural selection or by species selection—or by some combination of the two. We do not know whether both of them are important, or whether one of them is the main cause of evolutionary trends. Nor do we know the cause of the grand patterns of rise, fall, and replacement of groups. They may sometimes be random, and sometimes caused by the changing competitive advantages of different groups. When neither evidence nor probability favours one theory over another, there is nothing to be gained from attitudinizing. We should nail our colours, for the moment, to the fence.

Appendix: The Machinery of Molecular Genetics

The main agent of inheritance is a molecule called DNA (which stands for deoxyribose nucleic acid). For the purposes of this book it is necessary to know a little about DNA: its structure, how it causes bodies to be built, and how it is passed on from one generation to the next.

DNA is in almost every cell of the body. It is located in the cell in its own compartment, called the nucleus. Inside the nucleus the DNA is arranged in string-like structures called chromosomes (a chromosome consists only of DNA and some special proteins). Each cell contains a double set of chromosomes. The level of detail so far can be discerned in a microscope; but we must now move down to the submicroscopic level. The DNA molecule has the shape of a coiled double helix, like a spiral staircase seen when drunk. Each of the two coiled strands consists of a backbone of alternating molecules of sugar and phosphate, and attached to each sugar is the most important part, a kind of molecule called a base. There are four kinds of base, called (and symbolized) adenine (A), cytosine (C), guanine (G), and thymine (T). The DNA molecule is a chain made up of a sequence of the tripartite unit of sugar, phosphate, and base. The base is the only part that varies in the sequence, and a DNA molecule can informatively be described by its base sequence, such as ATGGCTTAC . . . The whole molecule is a double chain, in which complementary bases are opposite each other, C with G and A with T; the sequence of one of the chains therefore fully defines the sequence of the other (Figure 12).

The DNA molecule is a long set of instructions for building a body. The instructions are encoded in the exact base sequence. It is a simplification, but not for our purposes an over-simplification, to say that bodies are largely built by and of proteins; the other body constituents—fats and sugars—are metabolized, moved around,

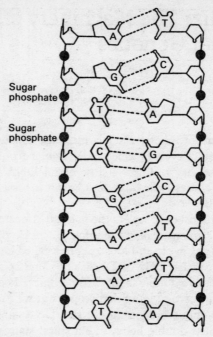

Fig. 12. The structure of DNA.

There is a backbone of alternating phosphate and sugar molecules, with a base (of which there are four kinds A, C, G, T) attached to the sugar. Two such chains, of complementary form and attached to each other, make up the whole DNA molecule.

and put in their place by proteins. Like DNA, proteins are long molecular chains made up of a sequence of building blocks; in proteins the building blocks are the 20 different amino acids. The properties of proteins are determined by their amino sequence.

The DNA base sequence encodes the amino acid sequence of proteins. The DNA is divided into units, called genes, that encode for one protein. The exact method of decoding is known. There are four bases, but twenty amino acids: each amino acid is encoded by a triplet of bases. The relation of which triplet encodes which amino acid is known, and is called the genetic code. The protein is actually made from an intermediary molecule, called mRNA. mRNA has a similar structure to DNA, one

2nd→ 1st↓	U	C	A	G	3rd↓
U	Phe Phe Leu Leu	Ser Ser Ser Ser	Tyr Tyr Non 2 (ochre) Non 1 (amber)	Cys Cys Non 3 Trp	U C A G
C	Leu Leu Leu Leu	Pro Pro Pro Pro	His His Gln Gln	Arg Arg Arg Arg	U C A G
A	Ile Ile Ile Met	Thr Thr Thr Thr	Asn Asn Lys Lys	Ser Ser Arg Arg	U C A G
G	Val Val Val Val	Ala Ala Ala Ala	Asp Asp Glu Glu	Gly Gly Gly Gly	U C A G

Fig. 13. The genetic code is written in triplets of bases.

There are four bases, and 64 possible different triplets. The amino acid encoded by each of the 64 is known. The full name of the amino acids has been abbreviated in the Table: UUU, for instance, encodes phenylalanine.

important difference being that mRNA has the base uracil (U) instead of thymine (T). The genetic code is customarily written for the mRNA code of A, C, G, and U (Figure 13). The main text of this work discusses two important points about the genetic code, that it is universal (p. 10) and redundant (p. 69). Thus, a particular gene will cause the same protein to be built in a bacterium as in a rabbit; this experiment indeed has been performed (and is, by the way, the basis of the modern technology of gene cloning). The code is redundant because there are 64 possible base triplets but only 20 amino acids; different triplets encoding the same amino acid are called synonymous. The length of a gene depends on the length of the protein it encodes; different proteins have very different lengths, but a typical figure is about 300 amino acids: a gene therefore is about 1,000 bases long.

The molecular mechanics through which a protein is made from a gene need not concern us. The double helix is uncoiled, a complementary intermediary molecule (called mRNA) is made, and another molecule (tRNA) recognizes the triplets of the mRNA and puts the appropriate amino acid against each triplet.

DNA is handed on to the next generation in special cells called gametes (sperms or pollen in the male, eggs or ovules in the female). Gametes, like other cells, contain chromosomes. At reproduction the double set of chromosomes has to be halved, because the offspring inherit an equal number of chromosomes from their male and female parents (therefore, if it were not halved, the number of chromosomes would double each generation *ad infinitum*). Sexual reproduction restores the double set. The special cellular cycle that produces gametes is called meiosis. We need not discuss its details, except to note that it is the occasion of genetic recombination. Recall that a chromosome is a string of genes; that each body contains two sets of genes (on two sets of chromosomes); and that, if a gene is in the heterozygous (p. 17) condition, its exact form will differ on the two chromosomes of a pair. At recombination, the pair of chromosomes move close to each other and physically recombine: each breaks at the same point, and they then join up with the strand of the other chromosome. If all the genes on the chromosome were homozygous, the chromosomes after recombination would be identical to what they were before. But because the majority of genes are heterozygous the recombined chromosomes usually contain a different set of genes from the parental chromosomes. This is one of the main reasons why offspring differ from their parents. (Mendelian segregation is the other.)

Mutations are the source of evolutionary novelties. They are changes in the structure of the DNA, which causes different proteins (and different bodies) to be made. There are several kinds of mutation. Large-scale chromosomal mutations are one: whole regions of chromosomes may be deleted, duplicated, inverted (p. 118), or transferred to another chromosome. The other main kind is the point mutation, in which in reproduction the wrong base is copied from the parental DNA. This may result in a change in one amino acid of a protein. All evolutionary changes start out as changes in genes. Their fate is then determined by natural selection or by luck.

Further Reading

Chapter 1

C. Darwin, *On the Origin of Species*, 1859.

Chapters 2 and 3

T. Dobzhansky, *Genetics of the Evolutionary Process*, 1970.
P. M. Sheppard, *Natural Selection and Heredity*, 4th edn., 1975.

Chapter 3

L. Margulis, *Symbiosis in Cell Evolution*, 1982.

Chapter 4

R. Dawkins, *The Selfish Gene*, 1976.
G. C. Williams, *Adaptation and Natural Selection*, 1966.

Chapter 5

M. Kimura, *The Neutral Theory of Molecular Evolution*, 1983.
R. C. Lewontin, *The Genetic Basis of Evolutionary Change*, 1974.

Chapter 6

M. Ridley, *Evolution and Classification*, 1985.

Chapters 7 and 8

E. Mayr, *Animal Species and Evolution*, 1963.

Chapters 9 and 10

J. Maynard Smith (ed.), *Evolution Now*, 1982.
B. Rensch, *Evolution above the Species Level*, 1959.
G. G. Simpson, *The Major Features of Evolution*, 1953.

Index

OXFORD

MORE OXFORD PAPERBACKS

Details of a selection of other books follow. A complete list of Oxford Paperbacks, including The World's Classics, Twentieth-Century Classics, OPUS, Past Masters, Oxford Authors, Oxford Shakespeare, and Oxford Paperback Reference, is available in the UK from the General Publicity Department, Oxford University Press, Walton Street, Oxford, OX2 6DP.

In the USA, complete lists are available from the Paperbacks Marketing Manager, Oxford University Press, 200 Madison Avenue, New York, NY 10016.

CHARLES DARWIN AND T. H. HUXLEY:
AUTOBIOGRAPHIES

Edited with an Introduction by Gavin de Beer

Charles Darwin and his 'Bulldog', T. H. Huxley, are presented here as each depicted himself. Two men of completely different temperament, they had immense admiration and respect for each other.

'It is singularly appropriate that these two autobiographies should be reprinted together, for in the history of science there can hardly have been a more fruitful and essential association of two men of such strikingly different personalities.' *Journal of Natural History*

'the fragmented autobiography which Darwin wrote for private circulation among his family is one of the most charming documents I have read in years' Benny Green, *Spectator*

DARWIN

Jonathan Howard

Darwin's theory that men's ancestors were apes caused a furore in the scientific world and outside it when *The Origin of Species* was published in 1859. Arguments still rage about the implications of his evolutionary theory, and scepticism about the value of Darwin's contribution to knowledge is widespread. In this analysis of Darwin's major insights and arguments, Jonathan Howard reasserts the importance of Darwin's work for the development of modern biology.

'Jonathan Howard has produced an intellectual *tour de force*, a classic in the genre of popular scientific exposition which will still be read in fifty years' time.' *Times Literary Supplement*

Past Master

GENESIS

The Origins of Man and the Universe

John Gribbin

The author begins his cosmic history some fifteen billion years ago, a split second after the 'big bang' of creation, and leads us on a fascinating voyage through vast reaches of time and space to the here-and-now of life on earth today.

'A splendid book.' Douglas Adams, author of *The Hitch Hiker's Guide to the Galaxy*

'Britain's answer to Carl Sagan? Comparisons between this latest work by John Gribbin and the much publicized *Cosmos* are inevitable and the comparison I found favourable to *Genesis*.' *Physics Bulletin*

GAIA

A New Look at Life on Earth

J. E. Lovelock

De Lovelock's Gaia hypothesis first took the scientific world by storm in the mid-seventies. He proposed that all living things on the earth are part of a giant organism, involving air, oceans, and land surface, which for millions of years has controlled the conditions needed for a healthy planet. While stressing the need for continued vigilance, Dr Lovelock argues that, thanks to Gaia, our fears of pollution-extermination may be unfounded.

'This is the most fascinating book that I have read for a long time.' Kenneth Mellanby, *New Scientist*

THE EXPANDING CIRCLE
Ethics and Sociobiology
Peter Singer

Where do ethical standards come from? Are our notions of good and evil created by reason, or by evolution? Can society shape its own destiny, or must it merely reflect biological imperatives? In answering these questions Peter Singer (author of the widely acclaimed *Animal Liberation* and, with Deane Wells, *The Reproduction Revolution*) is particularly concerned with the light thrown on our morality by the new science of sociobiology. He builds up a convincing picture of an ethical system which, though biologically grounded, has expanded from this base to become more rational and objective.

'Unwaveringly clear, rigorously accessible.' *Sunday Times*

AN INTRODUCTION TO THE STUDY
OF MAN

J. Z. Young

There are many ways of approaching the study of Man. Professor Young believes that biological knowledge provides a useful framework to help us to understand ourselves. Modern biology embraces many disciplines, and in this book a synthesis is made tracing the sources of human activity from their biochemical basis to the highest levels of consciousness.

'Professor Young sticks to straight and informative science . . . is rivetingly interesting, and conveys a constant sense of the controlled, critical curiosity which is what science is about.' *Guardian*

'an impressive performance' *Observer*

A SHORT HISTORY OF SCIENTIFIC IDEAS
TO 1900

Charles Singer

This book places the basic scientific ideas developed by man in a framework of world history, from the earliest times in Mesopatamia and Egypt until A.D. 1900, and treats not only the physical and chemical but also the biological disciplines. Published over 20 years ago to glowing reviews, it has become a standard work.

'One reason why this new history of science is assured of an illustrious career is that it is a work of such consummate art . . . masterly in conception and execution.' *New Scientist*

'this book is in the very front rank' *Advancement of Science*

'Dr Singer deserves well of Western man' *The Economist*